# MORE THAN REFUGE

SUELLEN MURRAY's interest in the women's refuge movement was born out of her involvement in feminist activism in the 1980s. She later completed her doctorate and taught women's studies and social sciences at Edith Cowan University. During this time, she was a board member of the Centre for Research for Women and a member of the Nardine Women's Refuge management committee. Since 2001, Suellen has worked as a researcher for the Victorian Community Council Against Violence and is a management committee member of a Melbourne women's refuge.

# MORE THAN REFUGE

## CHANGING RESPONSES TO
## DOMESTIC VIOLENCE

SUELLEN MURRAY

University of Western Australia Press

First published in 2002 by
University of Western Australia Press
Crawley, Western Australia 6009
www.uwapress.uwa.edu.au

Publication of this book was made possible with generous
funding assistance from the Lotteries Commission of Western
Australia, the Centre for Research for Women and Edith
Cowan University.

Western Australia
Millions Won. Thousands Helped.

National Library of Australia Cataloguing-in-Publication entry:

Murray, Suellen May.
    More than refuge: changing responses to domestic violence

    Bibliography.
    Includes index.

    ISBN 1 876268 83 2.

    1. Nardine Women's Refuge (W.A.).  2. Women's shelters—
    Western Australia.  3. Women's shelters—Western Australia
    —Case studies.  4. Family violence—Western Australia.
    5. Women—Services for—Western Australia.  I. Title.

362.838309941

Cover image: Domestic violence memorial march, Perth, 2002.
        Picture Jackson Flindell, *Sunday Times*
Produced by Benchmark Publications, Melbourne
Consultant editor Amanda Curtin, Curtin Communications, Perth
Index by Anne Batt, Perth
Designed by Ron Hampton, Pages in Action
Typeset in Adobe Garamond by Pages in Action, Melbourne
Printed by McPherson Printing Group, Maryborough

*For my mother and in memory of
my father (1921–2000)*

# Contents

# Acknowledgments

The history of responses to domestic violence in the late twentieth century has been largely undocumented. I was reminded of this gap in Western Australia's social history in 1997 after being elected to the newly formed management committee of Nardine Women's Refuge. As someone who had been involved in feminist political action in Perth, particularly during the 1980s, I was very aware of Nardine as a radical feminist institution that provided services to women and children escaping domestic violence. I became interested in using the history of this refuge as a case study in documenting the changing responses to domestic violence since the 1970s.

In 1997, Nardine was transforming into a hierarchical management structure after twenty-three years of operation as a collective—a significant (and controversial) milestone. Another approaching milestone was the refuge's twenty-five years of service provision, to be marked in 1999. I approached the then chair of the management committee, Lois Gatley, and other members and staff, who granted approval for me to access the refuge's archives and to proceed with the research. I wish to thank the management committee and staff for their willingness to allow me to undertake the project and for their ongoing interest and support. While I hope that this book goes some way towards meeting their expectations, it is my own work and is not written on behalf of Nardine.

Without the contributions of former workers and residents of Nardine and others from the wider field of domestic violence services and those with an interest in it, this book could not have been written. Even though Nardine houses a large and invaluable archive, the spoken words of the participants have enriched the book immeasurably. More than that, though, the enthusiasm of these people for the project has inspired and sustained me.

Supporting the publication of this book is funding from the Lotteries Commission of Western Australia, the Centre for Research for Women and Edith Cowan University. In addition, Edith Cowan University fostered the project through approval for academic study leave and funding for two projects that contributed to the research. I wish to thank the staff of these organizations, including Elizabeth Reid Boyd and the board of management of the Centre for Research for Women, and Sherry Saggers and Bill Louden from Edith Cowan University, for their faith in my ability to write this book.

Thanks are also due to those who assisted me in locating sources. Karin Hoffman at Lespar Library and staff at the State Records Office, the J. S. Battye Library of Western Australian History, the Supreme Court of Western Australia archives, Edith Cowan University libraries, Murdoch University Library Special Collection, the Western Australian Parliamentary Library and the *West Australian* newspaper photographic library all provided valuable assistance.

I wish to thank friends and colleagues who have supported me along the way, including Alanna Clohesy, Judi Cowie, Deborah Dearnley, Leonie Gibbons, Annie Goldflam, Jan Grant, Lekkie Hopkins, Graham McKay, Elizabeth Reid Boyd, Eversley Ruth, Sherry Saggers, Margaret Sims, Diane Snooks and Pamela Weatherill. Delys Bird, Trish Crawford and Pen Hetherington have mentored me academically and I thank them for their encouragement and guidance. Students whom I have taught at Edith Cowan University have helped me to make sense of many issues, and I acknowledge their contributions to my own learning and thank them for their interest in this project. Amanda Curtin has been a generous and patient editor and I am grateful to have had the benefit of her expertise. Finally, I warmly thank Trish Crawford, Lois Gatley and Helen Wildy, who generously and thoughtfully read earlier drafts of the book, and Libby Best, who both read earlier drafts and magnanimously maintained her interest in and support of my work throughout the project.

Suellen Murray

# List of abbreviations

| | |
|---|---|
| CASH | Crisis Assistance, Supported Housing (Award) |
| SAAP | Supported Accommodation Assistance Program |
| WCAG | Women's Centre Action Group |
| WCTU | Women's Christian Temperance Union |
| WEL | Women's Electoral Lobby |
| WESP | Women's Emergency Services Program |

# Introduction: Making the personal political

> The new [women's] movement demanded equality and justice
> for women more aggressively than had its predecessors; it developed a
> more thorough critique of existing society and the processes of male
> domination, and sought to empower women by changing their assumptions
> about themselves and their aspirations, dreams and abilities.
> ANN CURTHOYS, 1992[1]

'The personal is political' was not just a powerful feminist slogan of the 1970s; it was also a guiding philosophy of the women's liberation movement that assisted in making public a range of issues, such as childbirth, contraception and sexuality, that were largely considered private before this time. While feminists believed that the personal was political and that private matters had public implications, they had to work hard to encourage others to appreciate their point of view.

This book explains how feminists transformed domestic violence, which was considered to be personal and private three decades ago, into a public issue requiring political action and substantial government resourcing of human service responses. Perhaps feminists' success in achieving this outcome should not be considered surprising given that an estimated one-quarter of Australian women experience domestic violence.[2] However, what *is* surprising, and both puzzling and appalling, is that such an important issue for women, children *and* men was ignored for so long. Now domestic violence is a major social issue addressed by Australian governments, and has been identified as a high priority across all sectors of the Western Australian Government. In economic terms, it is estimated that domestic violence costs the Australian community, directly and indirectly, more than $1.5 billion a year in such areas as medical services, accommodation services, legal services, income provision, court and corrective services, and foregone income and lost productivity.[3] Ironically, in these times of economic rationalism and the overriding concern with the market economy, it seems as though the financial impact of domestic violence has contributed to its rise on the political agenda. But this issue cannot be measured in economic terms alone. The emotional, physical and social impact of violence on women and children is immeasurable.

Despite the increased community awareness of and government action concerning domestic violence from the 1990s, there has been little historical analysis of responses to domestic violence in Western Australia or elsewhere in Australia. No full-length histories of Western Australian refuges or other services in this field have been written. The existing body of international literature indicates that although there is interest in the topic, there are substantial gaps in research.

The central themes of this book are the emergence and activities of the movement against domestic violence from the mid-1970s, and the subsequent responses by the government and the community. The case study of Nardine Women's Refuge,[4] established in 1974 as Western Australia's first feminist refuge, provides an opportunity for analysing the background of and motivations for these responses, and how they changed over time. Nardine was not the *first* service to provide accommodation to women and children escaping domestic violence. Indeed, it was preceded by three other refuges—the Salvation Army's Graceville, the Catholic Church's Ave Maria and Fremantle City Council's Warrawee—the first of which was established in the late nineteenth century. However, the significant difference is that while these other three organizations accommodated women and children in crisis, Nardine was the first to identify specifically the circumstances of domestic violence from which they sought refuge.

This book demonstrates the impact of feminism on the provision of services in the field of domestic violence by showing how feminist practice informed theory in developing understandings of domestic violence.

## DEFINING DOMESTIC VIOLENCE

Before the 1970s, 'domestic violence' was not a term and barely a concept. The creation of the term by feminists during the 1970s reflects a change in attitude from acceptance to resistance in relation to the abuse of women within and after marriage and intimate relationships. While other names have been used, such as 'spouse abuse' and 'wife battering'—and, in the language of pre-1975 divorce applications, 'cruelty'—'domestic violence' has most consistently been used in the last three decades in Western Australia. In recent years, the term 'family violence' has been introduced, to refer specifically to Indigenous women and their extended families' experiences of violence; this term is preferred by the Indigenous community. This book adopts the term 'domestic violence' generally and 'family violence' when discussing Indigenous people specifically.[5]

The definition of domestic violence is not uncontested. It has changed over time and in differing political contexts. In 1997, the Australian Heads of Government National Domestic Violence Summit defined domestic violence as

> an abuse of power perpetrated mainly (but not only) by men against women both in relationship or after separation. Domestic violence takes a number of forms, both physical and psychological. The commonly acknowledged forms of domestic violence are physical and sexual violence, emotional and social abuse and economic deprivation.[6]

In Western Australia, recent State programs concerning domestic violence have used the broader definition adopted in 1992 by the National Committee on Violence Against Women:

> Domestic violence is considered to be behaviour which results in physical, sexual and/or psychological damage, forced social isolation, economic deprivation, or behaviour which causes the victim to live in fear.[7]

In recent years, the debate about domestic violence has also widened. There is now discussion about violence by women against men in intimate relationships.[8] In these situations, what constitutes violence needs to be carefully considered given the differing gendered contexts in which it occurs. There is also debate about violence in lesbian and gay relationships, and at least one Australian State has widened violence restraining order legislation to include same-sex relationships.[9] One of the effects of this widening of the debate about domestic violence is to challenge radical feminist analyses that rely on gendered power differences as the underpinning explanation for it. While noting the significance of these debates about other forms of violence in intimate relationships, this book focuses specifically on the development of responses to men's violence against women and children. Over 90 per cent of reported incidents of domestic violence are committed by men against women.[10]

## POWER, PATRIARCHY AND RADICAL FEMINISM

In the 1970s, when understandings of domestic violence were being developed, several strands of feminism were in existence or emerging. However, the underpinning ideas of radical feminism were those best able to make sense of male violence against women.[11] Radical feminism was characterized by the understanding that society was patriarchal, or male-dominated, and that men as a group had greater power than women had. This could readily be demonstrated by male dominance of social institutions such as the law, medicine and education, as well as in the family. According to radical feminists, this dominance was partly due to men's control of women's bodies, as manifested, in particular, in violence against women.

The radical feminist position was underpinned by a belief that the different lived experiences of men and women required a politics that took that difference into account. Women's experiences of their bodies in relation to, for example, childbearing, mothering, sexuality and violence had to be recognized. In contrast to the liberal feminists' desired goal of equality, defined in terms of predetermined masculine norms, radical feminists argued that women's different embodiment was centrally important.

How difference was understood within radical feminism varied. Some radical feminists favoured a biological basis—that is, acknowledging that there were fixed ways of being men and women, and that maleness and femaleness, masculinity and femininity, were immutable. Others believed that the patriarchal society in which they lived was socially constructed. The latter approach was paramount for those radical feminists among the refuge movement campaigning for social change. Although they accepted that there were real effects of living in a patriarchal society, such as women's and children's experiences of domestic violence, they were not convinced that patriarchy was fixed in any way. Their political actions were a testament to their belief that it could be otherwise. So while they spoke of a 'male-dominated society' and worked with the impact of the aggressive masculinity of domestic violence that was seemingly biologically determined, they believed that maleness, masculinity and patriarchal society could each be something else. Similarly, women who participated in consciousness-raising groups in the 1970s were able to reinterpret their experiences of family life, including, for some, domestic violence, as the available discourses shifted to include feminist understandings of gendered power differences within the family. Again, they believed that change was possible.

Radical feminism was centrally concerned with the exercise of power. The activities of the feminists described in this book indicate this concern, as well as their understanding that resistance was possible. The processes of resistance could be seen in the naming of domestic violence, the setting up of refuges, the promotion of the empowerment of women and children, and a range of other protest mechanisms. At the same time, feminists argued that the capacity to exercise power and to achieve desired effects has a political context. There are, they contended, gendered power differences related to the respective positions of men and women in society.

Before 1974, dominant discourses in Australia produced particular attitudes towards domestic violence that served the interests of men. From 1974, an alternative discourse developed, based on radical feminist practices responding to women's and children's experiences of domestic violence, and by the late 1990s this had been incorporated into government policy and, to some extent, human service practice. This book shows how this shift in power occurred.

Radical feminism assumed, in some senses at least, commonalities among women, as elaborated in the concept of 'sisterhood'. The concept of 'woman' was to become increasingly problematic as class, ethnicity, sexuality and other social categories cut across gender to complicate the possibility of sisterhood and women's shared goals. Thus, in more recent times, some forms of poststructuralist feminism have suggested that the concept of 'woman' should be dissolved. However, the radical feminists whose stories are told in this book were clearly convinced of the reality of the existence of 'women' as a homogeneous group. It was, for example, women with whom they worked who experienced domestic violence. For some, especially during the 1980s, those who were more 'women-identified' were considered to be the most authentic. For example, among those who pursued lesbian separatist forms of radical feminism, there was a belief in a fixed essence of womanhood that could be discovered or created through the development of a women-only subculture. Not all radical feminists took this approach. Some, speaking retrospectively, would describe their understandings of femaleness and femininity as being not biologically determined but discursively produced.

Similarly, feminist historians Patricia Grimshaw, Marilyn Lake, Ann McGrath and Marian Quartly, in the introduction to their Australian history *Creating a Nation*, recognized the complexity of the category 'woman':

> There are none who live only or purely as women. Rather, women experience the world as lesbian women and as white women, as Italo-Australian women and as working-class women, as mothers and as Aboriginal women…The meaning of femininity is never fixed and always contested.[12]

However, they do not agree that there are 'no real women or that their reality cannot be known or is of little interest'. Indeed, their project, and mine, 'pays tribute to and is crucially dependent on the past labours and insights of countless real women'.[13]

## ORGANIZATION OF THE BOOK

This book aims to place responses to domestic violence within their historical context. It acknowledges the work of Nardine Women's Refuge and other refuges in relation to domestic violence and also reminds us of feminists who came before them and laid the groundwork for those of the 1970s. Chapter 1 presents the background to the Western Australian women's movement from the late nineteenth century to the early 1970s, outlining 'protectionist' attitudes and strategies towards women and children who experienced domestic violence and the significant change that occurred when the framework became one of empowerment. Understandings of women's political activity in the earlier decades of the twentieth century are informed by Australian historian Marilyn Lake's concept of 'maternal citizenship' and her analysis of the shifts in feminist activity around difference and equality between men and women.

Chapter 2 discusses the beginnings of the international movement against domestic violence in the 1970s and the work of members of the Perth women's movement to establish Nardine Women's Refuge. The third chapter considers the ways in which a developing radical feminism was enacted at the refuge. This included work to promote the empowerment of women, the support of children, collectivity and women-identification.

At the same time that feminists worked with women and children affected by domestic violence, they were also making sense of it. Exposure to the extent and severity of domestic violence informed these women's theorization of the issue. Chapter 4 discusses a history of understandings of domestic violence, starting from its appearance in Western Australian divorce laws as 'cruelty' in the 1860s through to 1990s feminist understandings based on power and control, informed by the work of refuges from the 1970s.

Chapter 5 considers responses to domestic violence in the 1980s, focusing on the activities of the Western Australian Labor government's

Domestic Violence Task Force. Its report, *Break the Silence*, began to bring about increased coordination of and improved responses to domestic violence, built upon the lobbying work of feminist refuge activists that had occurred for over a decade.

During the 1990s, responses to domestic violence proliferated. Chapter 6 surveys and analyses the range of services and programs established. The book's Conclusion reflects upon the extent of social change in relation to domestic violence and considers implications for the future.

# From protection to empowerment: A background to feminist politics

> …women have equal access to the law, but what if its categories, constructs and interpretations are based on men's experiences of the world? Women now have, for the most part, equal access to the professions and public life, but what if these have been built around the assumption that their occupants are free from the responsibilities of children and daily life? Women are eligible to sit in the national parliament, but what if the founding fathers chose to locate it hundreds of kilometres away from the cities where most people live with their families? Women are now free to go out into the world as independent citizens, but what if the pervasive fear of male violence keeps them shut indoors?
>
> MARILYN LAKE, 1999[1]

Australian historian Marilyn Lake points to the limitations of a feminism based on equality. Instead, a recognition of the different life experiences of men and women demands a feminism that recognizes and articulates sexed differences. In this story of changes surrounding domestic violence, changing feminist politics of equality or difference is a significant thread. For those who pursued a politics of difference, the understanding that the private world was inherently linked to the public was paramount.

Feminist politics concerned with sexed differences were evident from the late nineteenth and early twentieth centuries. Feminists of both the 1890s and the 1970s understood that the personal was political. These groups of feminists, and others in between and since, believed that domestic violence was not a private matter but rather a serious public issue that required social change. But feminists of the latter decades of the twentieth century had considerably greater political, social and economic rights than did those of a century before. Thus, they were much more able to bring about change through political pressure. Furthermore, although feminists of the earlier years recognized that the personal was political, they believed that women's place was in the home. Later generations of women challenged this separation.

This chapter considers two questions. First, what was the background to the women's movement and feminist activism concerning what came to be called 'domestic violence' prior to the 1970s? Second, how can we explain the level of feminist activity concerning domestic violence since the mid-1970s? To answer these questions, we need to look at the history of feminism and to consider the changing context of women's lives in Western Australia.

## PROTECTIONIST FEMINISM

During the late nineteenth century, women's position in society was very different to that in the 1970s, as were the circumstances in which feminists attempted to bring about social change. Women were disadvantaged by both social expectations and legal regulations and were denied many of the citizenship rights afforded to men. Any property a woman owned at marriage was transferred to her husband. If she earned an income, it was considered to be her husband's. Custody of children lay with husbands. Women did not have sovereignty over their own bodies: through marriage, men had sexual access. Women could not vote (until 1899 for non-Indigenous women in Western Australia) or sit in parliament. Many jobs were denied to them, and when they were in the paid work force, their wages were considerably less than men's for the same or comparable work. There was extremely limited economic and social support available to women if they were deserted or had to leave a marriage because of domestic violence, or what was commonly called 'cruelty'. Women were expected to raise children and care for the family, and men to protect and maintain the family economically. However, this did not always happen, nor were women necessarily satisfied with the life that these limited citizenship rights and restrictive social expectations afforded.

In response to social, economic and legal restrictions, Australian feminists of the late nineteenth and early twentieth centuries worked towards 'maternal citizenship'.[2] As a product of their own social and political environment, they believed that women should be the 'mothers of the nation', that the care and comfort that they brought to the home as mothers could constructively be taken to the wider society. To do this, they had to gain certain rights, and hence they struggled for the vote so that women would have the opportunity to participate in the governance of the state and nation. Furthermore, they argued that, as mothers, women should be economically independent, to 'free them from demeaning dependence on husbands', and they appealed to the state 'to provide protection from predatory and exploitative men'.[3] At the same time, they argued that motherhood should be protected and valued.

Early feminists understood women in terms of their mothering. Women were defined as different from men. Either inherently or through their upbringing, they had different skills and qualities from those characteristic of men. Feminists of the late nineteenth and early twentieth centuries believed that womanhood embodied a range of positive qualities to which men should aspire—in other words, that men should be more like women. This is perhaps a surprising goal, because in more recent times we so often hear equality expressed in terms of women being equal to men—that is, that women should be more like, or have the same rights as, men. An introductory discussion, then, about changing conceptualizations of feminist goals will help make sense of how feminists tackled domestic violence and other issues over the twentieth century.

According to early feminists, within the private world of home and family, women and children needed protection, by virtue of their dependence:

> The conceptions of citizenship formulated by post-suffrage feminists in Australia were profoundly embodied articulations. They came from, and spoke to, the historical experience of women for whom heterosexuality was equated with violation and degradation…What was most material to feminists about women citizens' bodies was their violability and vulnerability.[4]

Women's 'violability and vulnerability' were experienced through sexual violence both inside and outside marriage, prostitution, unwanted pregnancy and venereal disease. Campaigns such as those opposing prostitution and those supporting the raising of the age of consent, the appointment of female public officers to deal with women and children, censorship of films and women's economic independence attempted to protect women (and children).[5] These campaigns contributed to the development of an Australian maternalist welfare state.

As well as protecting women and children and their position in the family, women's actions within the wider political world were aimed at maintaining difference.[6] In much later times, difference would again become a focus of feminism, but it would have other resonances.

In the earliest years of feminism in Western Australia, a number of individuals and organizations were actively seeking social changes beneficial to women from within this protectionist framework. The Women's Christian Temperance Union (WCTU) and the Karrakatta Club, for example, were active in promoting the female franchise, believing that women, through gaining the vote, would have greater power to effect change in other areas, including domestic violence. Although women's suffrage was clearly about gaining equal rights in political power, it was also about recognizing women's differences and ensuring that women were protected and achieved the political outcomes they sought.[7]

The WCTU was established in Western Australia in 1892, having originated in the United States in 1874. These women were an example of Lake's 'maternal feminists', seeing themselves very much as taking feminine values to the wider world:

> It was not enough they said for women to be home makers, they must make the world itself a larger home and protect mankind as they would their own families from spiritual, moral and social degradations.[8]

According to the WCTU, alcohol consumption was the cause of these 'spiritual, moral and social degradations', and the organization's ultimate goal was to achieve a temperate society. It identified poverty and violence as two outcomes of intemperance. The WCTU argued that alcohol prohibition was particularly important for women because it was women and children who were dependent on men and most keenly felt the effects of drunkenness.

Others also aspired to a temperate society and made links between alcohol consumption and women's disadvantage. Ada Bromham, an unsuccessful feminist candidate in the 1921 State election for the seat of Claremont, campaigned for alcohol restrictions during World War I through the Women's National Movement. This group later merged with the influential Women's Service Guild organization, which added prohibition to its platform.[9] Bromham campaigned under a banner stating:

> Women will help to create protective legislation for the factory, for the home and as between nation and nation, because they belong to the great human movement which includes equally men and women.[10]

Like Bromham and the WCTU, Edith Cowan appealed to the state for protective legislation to enhance the welfare of women and children. Cowan was the first woman to enter the Western Australian (and any Australian) Parliament, in the same election in which Bromham had been unsuccessful. Cowan had a long history of involvement in feminist and other organizations such as the Karrakatta Club, the Women's Service Guild, the National Council of Women and the Children's Protection Society. She had been active in seeking to improve the status of women and children through the development of services such as the women's hospital and kindergartens. Later, Cowan was to sit as a justice of the peace in Perth's Court of Petty Sessions and hear women's requests for judicial separation, a precursor to divorce, on the grounds of their husbands' cruelty. Cowan had known violence in her own life. When she was 7 years old, her mother had died in childbirth, after which she was sent to a boarding school. Her father, Kenneth Brown, remarried and in 1872 murdered his second wife.[11] As Cowan's biographer, Peter Cowan, explains:

Kenneth Brown believed his wife was having affairs with other men…She in turn charged him with heavy drinking…After a day of quarrelling and a long period of drinking, Kenneth Brown shot his wife.[12]

During her own marriage, Edith Cowan was again exposed to domestic violence, initially through her interest in her husband's work as a magistrate in the Perth Police Court, and later through her own involvement as a justice of the peace. In these earlier years, Cowan would have been made aware of cases such as this one in the 1890s:

In the Perth Police Court a man was charged with committing an aggravated assault on his wife, by beating her in the face with a red-hot iron bar. The bar had been placed in the fire, removed by wrapping one end with a piece of paper, and used as a weapon with enough effect to need a surgeon to sew the woman's lip.[13]

In this case, the prosecution of the husband was atypically undertaken by the police after the woman withdrew her complaint. Subsequently, the magistrate gave what was considered at the time an unusually severe punishment. This case was particularly noteworthy because, as was often the case, violence against wives was not considered a serious offence. In a discussion about the case in the *Daily News*, it was noted that 'for an assault on another man's wife a severe sentence was likely, but ill treating his own wife was too often regarded as exercising a sort of marital right'.[14] It was in this social and political environment that Edith Cowan and other feminists of the early twentieth century (and later) attempted to bring about change.

The Women's Service Guild (later Women's Service Guilds) took up this concern with the 'trivial punishments meted out in cases of assault' against women and children.[15] The Women's Service Guild was a remarkable Western Australian feminist organization that commenced in 1909 and was instrumental in initiating and supporting numerous significant social changes for women. Its campaigns included those that resulted in the establishment of the Perth women's hospital, improvements in the conditions for women prisoners, the appointment of women police and women justices of the peace, the setting up of free kindergartens and a training college for their teachers, and the formation of organizations such as the Association of Civilian Widows and the Slow Learning Children's Group. Through its national affiliation with the Australian Federation of Women Voters, it also campaigned for equal pay, the right of married women to work, women's eligibility for jury service and equality in training and job opportunities for women.[16] The Women's Service Guild took a typically liberal feminist approach in aiming for social reform to achieve equality for women.

Feminists of this early period, through a concern with the goals of maternal citizenship, were strongly supportive of women's economic independence. Jean Beadle was a founding member of the Labor Women's Organization in Victoria and, in 1905, of the Women's Labor League (later the Labor Women's Organization) in Western Australia. On the one hand, Beadle believed that women's place was within the home, but on the other she recognized that women would enter paid work and argued that they should receive equal pay to men.[17] Other post-suffrage feminists sought to achieve greater economic independence for women through such means as the maternity allowance and child endowment.[18] What these strategies attempted to do was to provide women with some capacity to support themselves economically and to reduce their dependence on men, while retaining the significance of maternity and difference.

Early feminists were particularly concerned about women's vulnerability to sexual violence, both inside and outside marriage. Only as recently as the 1980s and 1990s was legislation outlawing rape in marriage enacted in Western Australia and other Australian States. Before this time, men's conjugal rights provided for sexual access to wives in return for the economic maintenance of women and children. For these earlier feminists, citizenship rights for women included having the power to control their own bodies, including the right to refuse men's unwanted sexual advances. They believed that men should reform, to become more moral and sexually pure like women.[19] Men's unrestrained sexual behaviour resulted in increasing dependence for women through the production of larger families and the potential for reproductive ill health.[20]

In Western Australia, protection of 'vulnerable' and 'violable' women in relation to domestic violence, although not named as such, began in the late 1890s. The first three refuges in Perth, which were opened over a time span of more than seventy years, can be placed within a protectionist framework. In 1895, the Salvation Army opened its first 'Rescue Home', originally called Cornelie, in East Perth for the 'poor and fallen ones of the Colony'. By 1896, forty-one 'girls' had stayed at the home, with over half having moved on to 'situations' and three returning to live with friends. Within two years, this service had outgrown its accommodation and moved to larger premises in East Perth. At the turn of the century, it also operated as a maternity home for unmarried mothers; later these women would be accommodated at an alternative service in North Fremantle. In 1974, the service, now renamed Graceville Women's Centre, officially opened as a purpose-built refuge for 'deserted wives or destitute women and children', another for lone women, and further accommodation for women with intellectual disabilities.[21]

Opened in 1961, more than sixty years after the Salvation Army home, the second service providing accommodation to 'homeless women' in Perth was Ave Maria, the Catholic Daughters of Charity's women's shelter. Its residents were described as 'needy' and 'homeless' and, like at Graceville, violence was not articulated as a reason for their destitution. Instead, it was the 'woman just out of gaol or the luckless girl dismissed from her job' who would no longer have to 'resort to park benches'.[22] In the late 1970s, Ave Maria was to employ a newly qualified feminist social worker, Lois Gatley, who, while working within the constraints of the religious institution, provided information to residents to assist them to take control of their lives.

The third service to which women experiencing domestic violence could turn was established by the Fremantle City Council in 1971 to provide 'occasional' shelter for 'homeless' women. It was clear from the work of Warrawee that violence in the home was a reason for women seeking alternative accommodation, but during the service's earliest years it was assumed that women would seek temporary respite and then return home. Like the other two refuges previously established in Perth, during the earliest years of the service's operation, women who sought alternative accommodation to their own home continued to be protected rather than empowered. However, from the mid-1970s with the impact of feminist understandings of domestic violence, Warrawee's response to women and children increasingly became oriented towards empowerment.[23]

## EQUALITY FEMINISM

Equality, fired by the campaigns for equal pay and access to 'men's jobs' during World War II, was a powerful framework within feminism through the middle decades of the twentieth century.[24] This liberal feminist framework can be understood as an assimilationist model because the differences between women and men, such as women's reproductive capacity and child rearing responsibilities, were played down. Instead, men's position was constructed as the norm and feminist activity was directed towards achieving the same rights for women.

Equality is an inadequate goal of feminism, as it assumes that women will gain only what has already been predetermined from within masculine frameworks. It assumes that maleness is appropriately normative and that women should become like men to achieve equality. It has meant 'participating on men's terms'.[25] Thus, during the middle decades of the twentieth century:

> aspects of women's experience specific to women—childbirth, motherhood, sexual violation, domestic servitude of the wife, birth control—would gradually disappear from the feminist agenda, to be discovered anew in the 1970s when Women's Liberation declared the personal to be political.[26]

In particular, women's economic independence as citizen workers was sought. Sexual difference was minimized, and in feminist campaigns women were characterized as workers like men rather than as mothers.[27] While child-care was an issue, it was considered not as a special right for mothers but as necessary so that women could engage equally with men in the paid work force. The emphasis of feminist activity moved from the protection of the private world of home and family to ensuring women's progress in the public world, where achievement was measured against masculine standards. Underpinning this was the belief that with economic independence came freedom from oppression. This change of feminist direction came out of partic-ular circumstances where women workers had been attacked for taking men's jobs, especially during the Depression and after World War II. Feminists therefore focused on women's right to paid work as well as on equal pay and, later, equal opportunity.[28] As noted, the Women's Ser-vice Guilds were particularly active in these campaigns.

There were other feminist groups in Perth during the middle decades of the twentieth century—for example, the Modern Women's Club, founded by Western Australian author and Communist Party member Katharine Susannah Prichard, and the Union of Australian Women, a group with strong left-wing leanings that campaigned for equal pay, peace and environmental issues. Madge Cope, a former member of the Modern Women's Club, recalled that 'gradually we got tired and failed to recruit new young members. We decided to close up when women's liberation was beginning here [in Perth]'. Cope became a long-term member of the Women's Electoral Lobby (WEL).[29] In the decades between the two world wars, activist women were also involved with other peace organizations such as the Women's International League for Peace and Freedom.[30]

While much feminist activity during these middle decades was devoted to women's economic independence through campaigns con-cerning paid work and peace, feminists also focused attention on the particular circumstances of women—for example, the payment of maintenance to deserted wives, the standardization of divorce laws and, later, the introduction of the Single Mothers' Benefit.[31] Women's sexu-ality continued to be framed largely within a feminist discourse of purity and morality. In particular, during the war, with the presence of large numbers of servicemen seeking sex, feminists were concerned about the public expression of sexuality, prostitution, contraception and venereal disease. Women's vulnerabilities and violabilities were clearly apparent, and feminists attempted to address the immorality of wartime conditions. They successfully requested more women police, opposed the regulation of prostitution and supported restrictions on the sale of contraceptives, while advocating the establishment of a family planning clinic. Women's sexual autonomy was not an issue but rather the desire to protect women as mothers.[32]

## EMPOWERMENT FEMINISM

From the early 1970s, feminists reassessed their politics of equality, and difference again emerged as a powerful concept within feminism. While some retained liberal feminist orientations, for others within the women's liberation movement, and in particular those interested in the developing radical feminism, the implications of women's embodiment became increasingly significant. Women's experiences of sexuality, reproduction, the family and violence were analysed. These feminists highlighted structural power differences within society and argued that aiming to make women equal to men would only entrench a social system that already disadvantaged women. Radical feminists challenged notions of equality with men where masculine norms were considered desirable.

Significantly, this latter version of difference was not so much about protecting difference but rather about empowering it—that is, promoting women's capacities as women (however defined) and working towards structural changes that would give women more power both personally and politically. Thus, in contrast to the earlier decades of the twentieth century, when those few services that did offer refuge to women were oriented towards protection from violent or drunken men, feminist refuges from the 1970s offered another sort of security and safety. They did offer protection to women, but they were also places where feminists attempted to provide an environment where women could discover choices, take control of their lives and become empowered. Nardine and other feminist refuges, and services such as women's health centres, were established within these frameworks.

During these latter decades of the twentieth century, the increasing participation by women in higher education and in the paid work force was accompanied by decreasing fertility, due at least partly to the introduction of the contraceptive pill in the early 1960s. Women were participating more in the public worlds of work and education and having smaller families than their mothers and grandmothers had had earlier in the century. These changing conditions, for middle-class women at least, provided the social environment in which change could occur.

# CHAPTER 2

# Establishing a feminist refuge: Nardine as a 1970s response to domestic violence

…with a lot of enthusiasm and goodwill…
MICHELE KOSKY, 1998[1]

In the latter decades of the twentieth century, domestic violence became a particular focus for feminists. What, then, were the circumstances in which feminists in the 1970s established services for women and children escaping domestic violence and campaigned further for political action and social change? This chapter outlines the Australian social and political context of the 1970s and discusses the circumstances in which Nardine and other feminist women's refuges were set up from 1974. It also shows how feminists of the 1970s began to articulate a radical feminist understanding of domestic violence based on difference and empowerment.

## A TIME OF SOCIAL CHANGE

In Australia during the 1970s, there were social changes that together offered greater hope to women living with domestic violence. The development of the women's liberation movement and the establishment of women's refuges were certainly two of these changes. The possibility of women's greater economic independence was also a contributing factor. The Single Mothers' Benefit was introduced in 1972; entitlement to it, however, was stringently assessed.

Although women were disadvantaged within the labour market in terms of the kinds of work they could undertake and their rates of pay, as well as by the limitations imposed by the care of children, some changes were occurring in the 1970s. In 1969, after long-fought campaigns, 'equal pay for equal work' was introduced. However, as few women did the same jobs as men, these new legislative changes affected only a minority of women. Other reforms followed in 1972 and 1974 that further attempted to break down the impact of the sexual division of labour through a greater consideration of the value of women's work and the extension of minimum wages to women.[2] Furthermore, all around Australia, women campaigned for child-care, and there was increasing provision of these services.[3]

There were significant changes in relation to the structure of the family during this decade. The introduction of the *Family Law Act 1975* had an impact on women's ability to leave violent relationships.[4] There were also significant demographic changes. Family size decreased after the baby boom of the postwar years, which for many women reduced the periods of time dedicated to child rearing.

Finally, with the election of the social justice oriented Whitlam Labor Federal Government in 1972, coming as it did after twenty-three years of conservative government, the women's movement had a sympathetic political environment. As Deborah Brennan has noted:

> Labor's mood was one of expansion and optimism. The new government regarded social welfare as a fundamental aspect of the well being of all citizens. It placed considerable emphasis on the provision of services (such as health, child care and education) which benefited a wide range of people.[5]

The government adopted policies that resulted in the funding of community-based welfare agencies and the development of women's health centres, child-care centres, women's refuges and legal services—all important services for women.

## WOMEN'S LIBERATION

The Australian women's liberation movement came out of working-class and trade unionist activism, university campuses, the new left and other radical political movements including those against the Vietnam War. In each of these forums, women found that although there was talk of equality, women seemed to be excluded. Sexism and discrimination were rampant, and women involved in these groups rebelled. The beginnings of an emerging international radical feminist literature further fired women, and women's liberation groups were formed in 1970 in Sydney, Adelaide and Melbourne.[6] This much-discussed literature included radical feminist analyses of the family and heterosexuality, returning to themes previously perceived as private. The term 'patriarchy', or male domination, introduced through Kate Millett's *Sexual Politics*, became an important concept for feminists attempting to explain the structural and systemic disadvantage experienced by women. Germaine Greer's *The Female Eunuch* provided guidance in more individualistic ways in relation to dealing with feminine 'conditioning' and the impact of 'sex roles'.[7]

Women's liberation aimed to bring about personal and social transformation. An important tool of women's liberationists throughout Australia and elsewhere was consciousness-raising groups, in which women talked together about, among other matters, the difficulties of family life. It was through these groups that women developed their sense of the ways that the personal was political as they became aware of the commonality of their most private experiences. Consciousness-raising groups were not only opportunities to share experiences; they also informed feminist analysis and social action.[8] Cheryl Meinck explained the significance of consciousness raising to women's liberation, and the subsequent action:

> Women's Lib. in Perth began like that—exploded into life as we discovered our common oppression. By exchanging experiences, we gained a feeling of confidence, of solidarity and a rising anger

at the roles we were being forced to play. We had meetings, guerilla theatre and group action—all concerned with two vital aspects of change

1. educating ourselves
2. educating others (especially those with the power to change our situation).[9]

Pat Giles recalled the arrival in Perth of the women's liberation movement in the early 1970s:

It must have been in 1972 when notices suddenly started appearing up all over the place—'WOMEN'S LIBERATION—Inaugural Meeting!' There was a meeting of about forty or fifty young women and a sprinkling of young males at a home in Rivervale. We planned then for a big public meeting and that was held in April at the Trades Hall and between 400 and 500 people attended the meeting.[10]

From 1972, Women's Liberation held meetings on Sunday nights in the Youth Hostels rooms in Museum Street, Perth. At these meetings, consciousness-raising groups were run, films shown and discussions held about a range of feminist topics. During 1973, the movement had a meeting space in Subiaco, and in the later 1970s at other venues, including King Street, Perth, and Glendower Street, North Perth. *Liberation Information*, the Perth Women's Liberation newsletter, reported that the new feminist literature such as Germaine Greer's *The Female Eunuch*, Robin Morgan's *Sisterhood Is Powerful* and Kate Millett's *Sexual Politics* were for sale and that 'stimulating discussions' were taking place.[11] Other women were invited to participate:

Cultural customs, possible origins of women's oppression, the necessity for freely available abortion and other matters were discussed in a friendly atmosphere. Consciousness raising is an important part of the movement and discussion gives opportunity to have your say. Come and join us.[12]

A rally in Perth in 1976, organized by the Women's Electoral Lobby, protesting against cuts to women's services and calling on the newly elected Fraser government to honour election promises. *Courtesy* West Australian

Women's liberationists were also forging political alliances with other Perth feminists. In 1972, women linked with the loosely defined Women's Liberation group and the Harvest Guild, a member organization of the Women's Service Guilds, lobbied candidates for the federal election, as WEL women did in the Eastern States of Australia. As well, several, including Pat Giles, unsuccessfully stood for local government elections in 1972 on women's rights platforms. In March 1973, joined by others from the Harvest Guild, women's liberationists formed the first Western Australian branch of WEL, with Giles as the inaugural convenor.[13] As the formation of WEL suggests, there was considerable overlap in the membership of feminist organizations in Perth at this time. WEL was committed to taking action to improve the status of women through non-party political lobbying. It sought to 'change social attitudes and practices which discriminate against women' and operated through action groups including those that campaigned for abortion reform, child-care and equal pay.[14] Domestic violence was not an articulated area of concern at this time, as WEL's focus was on the public rather than private realm.[15]

In May 1974, Elizabeth Reid, the Women's Adviser to the then Prime Minister, Gough Whitlam, visited Perth to discuss the forthcoming provision of Commonwealth grants for women's services during 1975, the United Nations' International Women's Year. Michele Kosky, a founding member of Nardine, while not at that meeting, recalled that Reid had given women a challenge: 'that we should get ourselves together and start providing women-focused services for women'.[16] Reid spoke of 'the refuge set up in the East'.[17] Following the meeting, Sally Speed, Penny Fogarty, Diane Fruin, Michele Kosky and Helen Shannon came together to discuss suitable projects. There was considerable enthusiasm and energy. This group of women, with others who joined them, became the Women's Centre Action Group (WCAG). They decided to pursue the development of two women's services—a refuge, soon to become Nardine Women's Refuge, and a women's health service, the Women's Health and Community Centre (later to become Women's Health Care House)—both to be run on feminist principles.[18]

In setting up the refuge in Perth, these women were responding to the almost invisible social issue of domestic violence.

## THE BEGINNINGS OF THE 1970s MOVEMENT AGAINST DOMESTIC VIOLENCE

The refuge in Perth was developed within a context of international and national activism. In 1971, Erin Pizzey and a small group of women established a women's community centre in Chiswick in London. Their aim was to provide a venue for women with children to meet, to reduce their social isolation. The small house was named Chiswick Women's Aid. Its focus quickly became domestic violence, and women came from all over Britain seeking refuge from violent husbands.[19] As in Australia, welfare services then had little under-standing of the impact of domestic violence. In London, at a time when many women with children were financially dependent on their husbands, Pizzey reported that a woman would be informed that if she left her husband, she had 'voluntarily made herself homeless and therefore [was] not entitled to any assistance from social services'. It was not 'the policy of the social services to interfere with the sanctity of marriage'.[20]

Despite social welfare services' reluctance to assist, Chiswick Women's Aid overflowed with desperate women and their children. By May 1973, they were receiving 100 phone calls each day and accom-modating around thirty women and children at any one time. Later in 1973, they moved to a larger house and accommodated 130 women and children in a building licensed for thirty-six. Others heard about the project and set up similar houses elsewhere in Britain. Pizzey's book about domestic violence and the work of Chiswick Women's Aid, *Scream Quietly or the Neighbours Will Hear*, published in 1974, pro-voked international interest.[21] Anne Summers was thinking about set-ting up a refuge in Sydney after hearing of the work of Women's Aid from an article in 1973 in the feminist journal *Spare Rib*; she rang Pizzey and was told, 'just do it'—and, with others, she did.[22] At the time, Summers was involved in an array of political activism and was writing what was to become the classic Australian feminist text *Damned Whores and God's Police*. Even though she had been working on the manuscript for two years, 'it had not occurred to [her] to investigate violence against women'.[23]

In late 1973, Summers and her friend Jennifer Dakers were joined by a small group of women, and together they began planning the service. Unable to secure a house through legitimate ways, they found an unoccupied terrace house named 'Elsie' in Glebe, owned by the Church of England, and decided to set it up as the refuge and squat in it. As a result of interest provoked by a commission held on women and violence on International Women's Day in 1974, many more women found out about the planned Elsie Women's Refuge and offered to become volunteer workers. On 16 March 1974, Elsie, as well as the similarly unoccupied adjoining house, were broken into, their locks changed, the buildings cleaned and furnished, gardens tidied, and the words 'Women's Refuge' painted across the front walls. The refuge received considerable media attention and within several days the 'place was overflowing with women and kids'.[24]

Word spread. Within a couple of months of Elsie's opening, women began talking about opening a feminist women's refuge in Perth. Others were opening or being established in Melbourne, Adelaide and Canberra, and a year later there were eleven domestic violence women's refuges in Australia.[25]

## PLANNING PERTH'S REFUGE

In May 1974, at a WEL general meeting, Diane Fruin presented a request for WEL to join with Women's Liberation in writing a submission to apply for International Women's Year funds.[26] Women from these two groups and others formed the WCAG. Their aim was to set up a women's health and community centre that would comprise a health centre, a community centre and a women's refuge. Although the women's health centre took a little longer, these goals were achieved. Remarkably, within two months and with no government funding, the refuge was running.

The WCAG saw the planned Perth refuge as a place for 'women who need to get out of their marriage "homes", but have nowhere to take the kids while they look for their own place'.[27] The reason women had to leave their homes was identified from this earliest time of planning as due to an 'unbearable situation', to be elaborated in funding submissions as 'irrevocable incompatibility, mental and/or physical violence and cruelty'. Hence, domestic violence was very much a part of this group's understanding of women's 'homelessness' from the beginning. The refuge would be a 'warm and supportive' place where a woman would be 'treated in a respectful manner' and where she could 'help herself to get what she wants and, in the process, give support and receive it from other women who understand her situation because they've been in it too'.[28] The refuge would be based on self-help, a significant change from protection and a move towards empowerment.

In planning the refuge, the WCAG had to establish the need for such a service. In early 1974, the three existing refuges for homeless women, Warrawee, Graceville and Ave Maria House, were unable to keep up with the demand for emergency accommodation and turned away many women and children. For example, during the second half of 1973, Warrawee accommodated up to five women and their children at any one time, and had enquiries from a further three to five families each week.[29]

Clearly, there was a demand for further emergency accommodation. However, the WCAG was also concerned to provide a different kind of service. The existing services tended to operate under a protectionist model that provided respite only. It was assumed that women would leave violent relationships for periods of time but would return to them. In contrast, the planned refuge would actively work towards change on both personal and political levels. The WCAG would provide residents with information about leaving their abusive relationships and support them in carrying this out. Its approach was to foster self-help and an atmosphere in which women could take control of their lives. This model was consistent with those adopted elsewhere in Australian feminist refuges. Instead of the traditional hostel accommodation model, they provided services in a 'non-institutionalised and self-help environment, run by consumers and supporters of the refuge in a collective and consensual system'.[30] But the model was not only about providing services to women and children affected by domestic violence. The goals of the feminist refuges were much larger; they were about changing community understandings of domestic violence and reducing its incidence:

The model also called on refuges to use the experiences of the women and children residents to research and develop community awareness of domestic violence and homelessness, to uncover the root causes, which lay in women's oppression, and to demand an end to it. By doing so, the need for refuges would disappear thereby guaranteeing their obsolescence.[31]

With all these goals in mind, the WCAG took action.

## TAKING ACTION

In July 1974, with 'a lot of enthusiasm and goodwill', the WCAG began providing emergency accommodation in a small three-bedroom house in Vale Road, Mount Lawley.[32] From the original group of five women in May, it had grown by July to more than forty, who covered a twenty-four hour roster as volunteer workers at the refuge. The WCAG had attracted a mixed group, which, according to the *West Australian*, included

> students, teachers, social workers, a solicitor, office workers and housewives; though predominantly young, they range up to middle age and beyond; there are working wives and dependent wives, supporting mothers and single women; there are optimistic young idealists and practical realists.[33]

They had been brought together by

> concern for the welfare of women and determination to do something practical for women who suffer because society's attitudes have made them dependent and vulnerable…Help *for* women *by* women is the purpose. At the same time, they will show the rest of society the areas and the urgency of the need.[34]

And the need for their services was quickly realized. The Vale Road house experienced a 'flood of women' that 'never seemed to stop'.[35] There were never empty beds, and mattresses were routinely placed on the floor for women and children; when there was no room on the floor, 'overflow families' were accommodated in the homes of workers, ex-residents and volunteers.[36]

Many of the volunteer workers had little experience in welfare service provision, and the challenges and rewards were evident in this early report by Sally Speed, one of the founding members of the WCAG:

As we meet each crisis we are sustained by the thought that things can only get better as the routine becomes smoother…Many of our members have been quite inexperienced, but in line with the philosophy of self-help, the actual setting up and running of the house has contributed a great deal to the development of all the people involved.[37]

In November 1974, three months after opening, Nardine had accommodated thirty women and sixty children, social worker Pat Whitmarsh had been employed, and the WCAG was confident that funding would be forthcoming from the Commonwealth Government in 1975.[38] Optimism characterized its work:

The shelter is going really well and is turning into a very good community project. Some of the women are coming back on roster at the shelter, others keep in touch by phone calls and are coming to the Monday night meetings at WEL House.[39]

A month later, a second full-time worker, Gillian Draffin, was employed.

In its first year, from July 1974, Nardine accommodated 138 women, of whom seventy-nine were accompanied by children, and 172 children. Even more were turned away: 272 women, of whom 231 were accompanied by children, and 567 children. Over a third of these women had already tried the three other refuges in Perth at the time.[40] Even after Nardine increased the available emergency accommodation, this pattern continued. A quarterly report from the first year noted that the 'refusal rate continues to rise rapidly and we now turn away many families each week—sometimes up to four families per day!'.[41] In Nardine's contribution to the Royal Commission on Human Relationships undertaken in the mid-1970s, Gillian Draffin reported that the refuge was turning away three families for every one that it took in, confirming evidence from refuges across Australia that they were 'filled to overflowing'.[42]

In August 1975, after a year in Mount Lawley, the refuge moved to Vincent Street, North Perth. By this time, it had successfully secured funding from the State Health Department to employ five staff. These funds were shared among a larger number of workers who included Susie Wilkins (Strong), Colleen Hay and Gillian Draffin. The Vincent Street house was considerably larger, with six bedrooms, a community room, a small lounge, a dining room and an 'enormous' backyard. The refuge was soon to take on the adjoining property and, late in the 1970s, a third house in the next street. The refuge workers reported that although the Vincent Street house was 'bigger and brighter…it didn't take long before we were full to bursting and things were back to normal'.[43] Typically, families shared bedrooms. Deborah Dearnley, who worked at Nardine from the late 1970s, remembered the refuge as being 'very busy'. It is not surprising that Nardine was remembered in this way when the larger, six-bedroom Vincent Street house accommodated up to a dozen women and their children.[44]

Procedures were put in place to guide workers in helping residents. Workers were instructed to accompany women, as soon as possible, to the Department for Community Welfare, Legal Aid, the State Housing Commission, the Department of Social Security, the Health Department and their children's schools. They were to assist women to 'establish [their] credibility' as deserving welfare recipients and to clarify their situation under the *Family Law Act*. Thus, they worked with residents to begin proceedings to ensure legal separation, gain custody of children, receive maintenance and put in place non-molestation orders if required.[45]

During 1976, the WCAG attempted to draw supportive women into the movement for social change. Recognizing that 'many women [have] shown willingness to help but haven't had the opportunity to find out enough about the work', it ran a course to give women the feminist knowledge and practical skills to become volunteers at

Nardine and the Women's Health and Community Centre 'so that they could support other women effectively'. 'Caring feminists' were called upon to participate. In the Women's Liberation Involvement Course, as it was called, participants discussed the oppression of women and women's liberation. In addition, the course addressed issues such as women leaving home, wife beating, sexuality, rape and abortion. The processes of the movement, including self-help, consciousness raising and collectives, were also covered. Finally, information was provided about relevant agencies such as Community Welfare and the State Housing Commission.[46]

From these earliest days of the refuge, then, it is clear that the WCAG not only provided support and accommodation to women and children; it also lobbied for social change.

POLITICIZING DOMESTIC VIOLENCE

As Anna Spencer, a former Nardine resident and worker from the mid-1970s, remarked, 'it [the refuge] certainly was looking at the bigger picture stuff. It certainly wasn't just, "here you've got a roof over your head." It was a lot more than that'.[47] Having come out of the women's liberation movement, Nardine's feminists had the explicit goal of achieving social change:

> In groups of aware women, we can come and work together, and come to terms with the basis of our oppression, and work to change oppressive structures and attitudes.[48]

Having placed domestic violence within a wider social context, they attempted to work towards improving social structures that promoted gender equity. One of the explicit goals of the 1970s was to eliminate domestic violence. As Deborah Dearnley recalled, part of the refuge philosophy in the early days was 'to do ourselves out of a job'.

In the mid-1970s, the specific needs for social change became increasingly apparent. For example, around 1975 Nardine's feminists listed the following as targets for action:

a. [Writing a] Booklet 'what you need to know when you leave home'.
b. Getting the SHC [State Housing Commission] to stop building the awful types of flats and homes they have now.
c. Changing the attitudes of estate agents who will not let homes to women living on their own.
d. Fighting against the barriers placed by the Social Security that prevent women getting their rights.
e. Knowing the various problems women have met when dealing with the agencies, police courts, etc.[49]

The overall intention behind these goals remains important for the refuge movement today. For example, while the style of public housing has changed since the mid-1970s, decent and affordable long-term accommodation for women and their children after they leave a refuge is still a major issue.[50]

As planned, the WCAG was not only running the refuge (and working towards setting up the women's health service); during this time, it was also engaged in activities that attempted to bring domestic violence to the attention of the wider community. For example, during International Women's Year in 1975, women's refuges were in the spotlight. Nardine worker Gillian Draffin addressed the International Women's Day rally in Perth. She also attended the Women and Politics Conference in Canberra, a major event of International Women's Year, presenting a paper discussing the work of Nardine, and contributed to the Royal Commission on Human Relationships. In International Women's Day literature produced by Women's Liberation, domestic violence and women's refuges were mentioned as key issues. Nardine's workers were also involved in other forums where domestic violence was highlighted as an important community issue, including a seminar at the Fremantle Education Centre in 1976 and national women's refuge conferences commencing from 1978. During the earliest years of the refuge, Nardine workers often travelled interstate to meet with other refuge workers, to attend national refuge and other related conferences, and to lobby ministers and government officials.

Direct action was also taken, both to meet the immediate needs of women and children who had come to the refuge and to make a wider point about the need for such support and services for other women escaping domestic violence. As Sue Allen, a worker at Nardine in the late 1970s, recalled:

> We used to have difficulties trying to get allowances for women. I remember us once taking a whole group of women and children up to a departmental office…and not moving, refusing to move until we got something done. We literally sat there in their office…they asked us to move and we would say, 'No we're not moving. We've got these people who've got nowhere to go. They need assistance.'[51]

During the mid- to late 1970s, feminists were working in a hostile political environment. After Nardine, a number of other refuges quickly became established in Perth. Some, including Emmaus, started in 1976, were also feminist in their orientation. Michelle Scott was involved in setting up Emmaus and described the political environment at the time:

> There was a whole group of people, just volunteers, community people, who just decided to set up a refuge. We arranged the tenancy and rented a place in Nedlands. We worked all this weekend, we cleaned the place up, painted it, and we opened the doors. We got a call from the Health Department to say if we didn't shut the doors straight away we'd never get any funding…it was Charlie Court's electorate and there was no domestic violence in Nedlands or Dalkeith.[52]

Despite the lost time, money and effort put into setting up the refuge in one of the wealthiest suburbs of Perth, Emmaus went ahead, moving instead to the inner city. This reflects something of the conservative nature of the Western Australian Government of the late 1970s. The Premier, Charles Court, was reported to have said in a radio interview that 'the recipe for a successful marriage was a tolerant and patient wife'. Nardine and other like-minded feminist refuges were perceived as politically embarrassing, particularly as the Commonwealth was handing over refuge funding to the State during this time.[53] These perceptions were further confirmed by Ludo McFerran in her 1987 evaluation of women's refuges in Western Australia:

> It is unfortunate that in the past women's refuges in this state have conducted an essentially lonely battle to raise the issues of domestic violence and homelessness. An examination of the treatment of women's refuges in WA during the 1970s by the State Government and Administration tells a sorry tale of petty-minded and conservative thought.[54]

Not surprisingly, at this time Nardine was considered 'on the edge'. In the mid-1970s, Diana Warnock, then a volunteer at the refuge, recalled ringing the police to seek assistance because a woman was being attacked by her partner. Instead of complying with the request, police raided the refuge because it was believed that the women were 'drug taking hippies'.[55] Despite these community perceptions, there is evidence of support for refuges in State parliament. For example, in 1977 Keith Wilson, MLA, later to become the Minister for Community Welfare in the Burke Labor government, informed parliament that 'the five shelters for women operating in the metropolitan area are turning away possibly 250 women and children a month'. He asked what plans the government had to maintain existing shelters and to provide funding for more.[56] His information would have come from the refuges, and their lobbying ensured that the needs of women and children escaping domestic violence were beginning to be heard.

Nardine's developing understanding of domestic violence challenged others' views about the issue. As Sue Allen recalled, Nardine's feminists were politically radical:

> The staff in general were at various times a pretty radical lot...it went through periods where it was more radical or less radical but

you didn't have to be very radical in that time, at least as far as other institutions went, before it was outrageous…It was ground breaking…There was a lot of opposition in the community to the idea…It was like bringing the unspeakable out of the closet and [others] wanted to pretend that this was a minority thing that very rarely happened, and only through a few bad men. Whereas in fact we were demonstrating to society that this was a much broader problem and that it required a societal response not just an individual pathology type focus. And that it was in the context of gender-based power relations within society.

Despite opposition to the views expressed by Nardine's feminists and others in the refuge movement, they maintained their developing radical positions and persevered with political action:

And we wouldn't compromise in those early days, you know, we wouldn't put it in nice terms…And the fact that we started getting funding was pretty amazing. That was some demonstration of the extent to which we had an impact. But we did a lot of lobbying and a lot of requesting…[57]

Even though there were successes in terms of continued funding and the ongoing existence of the refuge, by about 1980 frustration was clearly evident:

I now recognize things won't change. The revolution is not only not imminent, it may in fact never happen. Wimmin and kids I knew three years ago are still on the same male social welfare refuge roundabout—Come to a refuge, get State Housing, get in arrears, get involved with a man who just might help out financially, pregnancy, evicted, back to the refuge…around and around…and this analysis doesn't even look at the many homeless wimmin who won't be accepted by refuges.[58]

The difficulty in working against wider social structures that disadvantaged women was also apparent at other Australian refuges.

Dianne Otto and Eileen Haley described the social context in which women came to the Adelaide Women's Shelter that, like Nardine, had opened in 1974. These women experienced a

> scarcity of cheap housing, [and] inadequate childcare and job opportunities. In addition, many women returned after a couple of days at the Shelter, to men who beat and generally mistreated them. We feel that this syndrome is likely to continue to happen, as long as present ideas about male/female relations continue to prevail—for example, that a woman needs a man, that no matter how bad he is she must stick by him, that self-sacrifice and suffering are feminine virtues, that children need a father (no matter how bad he is) etc etc.[59]

Despite frustration, political action continued throughout the 1980s.

GETTING FUNDED

The WCAG sought government funding to support its activities. Through its approach, it is clear that it identified Australia as a welfare state that was responsible for ensuring the safety and support of all its citizens, including women and children escaping domestic violence. In the Women's Liberation newsletter of June 1974, WCAG member Michele Kosky explained that 'we still need to pay our rent ($45/week) until the State and Federal governments recognise their responsibilities and give us a grant'.[60] Some women, however, were concerned about compromises that might be required if money were received from the patriarchal state. These concerns are evident in the WCAG's negotiations with the government regarding funding of the women's health service:

> The self-education process which members of the WCAG have gone through has been an eye-opener for many and for me, extremely interesting, worthwhile and involving but also bloody

frustrating, time-consuming, often very depressing and enervating. The joys were often an anticlimax and I feel that power of the enemy no. 1 (bureaucracy) is not to be underestimated…the fob-offs, misinformation and seemingly endless delays culminating in the likely failure of the project. In typical bureaucratic fashion our anger was defused by the dangling of carrots and assurances by our 'friends' in the bureaucracy that we might blow the delicate balance if we did anything 'silly'.[61]

Receiving funding meant that feminists had to be accountable, and accountability could be required in ways that were considered unacceptable or inappropriate. For example, in addition to annual audits, the Health Department insisted on refuge inspections. Over the following years, feminists continued to be concerned with the intrusion of the state into the work of the refuge, and resisted these interventions. However, at all times, government funding was accepted as a pragmatic solution that ensured the refuge was sustainable and was an acknowledgment that government was responsible for funding such services.

While it waited for the outcome of a submission to International Women's Year through the Department of Foreign Affairs, and others to the departments of Health and Social Security, the WCAG received a 'tremendous response' to its appeals for financial assistance.[62] By September 1974, over $2,300—enough to keep the refuge going—had been donated. Sources of the donations included the Lotteries Commission of Western Australia, the Women's Service Guilds, WEL, the Country Women's Association, the University of Western Australia Student Guild and personal pledges. The WCAG had thoughtfully requested individual donations of as little as 50 cents per week, which together had successfully paid the $45 per week rent for the first two months.[63]

By December 1974, Nardine had secured some funding from the State Department for Community Welfare to pay for one worker, the rent and some of the telephone bill. However, financial difficulties were never far away in these early months, and appeals were made in various forums, including, in February 1975, an article in the *Daily News* (see opposite). In March 1975, $3,000 (and a further $4,000 in June 1975) was received through the International Women's Year grants scheme. The Trades and Labor Council provided further funds, with individual unions such as the Clothing Trades Union, the Fire Brigade Union and the Hospital Employees Union also contributing; union support had been enlisted through the lobbying of Pat Giles, a union representative at the time and an active member of Women's Liberation. Other fund-raising avenues were also pursued. For example, in May 1975, Nardine held a fund-raising night at the Dianella Hotel. Finally, in June 1975, a year after Nardine had opened, ongoing funding was provided through the Commonwealth Government's Hospitals and Health Services Commission.[64]

The decision to fund refuges through the Hospitals and Health Services Commission was not without controversy. By June 1975, eleven refuges were in operation in Australia and all required secure funding to keep going. However, there was no existing government funding program that resourced the needs that refuges were addressing. It was a problem that had come to the attention of Elizabeth Reid, the Prime Minister's Women's Adviser, through refuge applications for International Women's Year funding. As Australian political scientist Marian Sawer explained, women's liberationists had expected that grants would fund newly developing women's services, but this program's priority was not ongoing funding. The already existing Home-less Persons Assistance Program did not address the needs of women and children escaping domestic violence. Other departments, including Social Security, were approached without success, although Reid believed that this department should take on the responsibility for refuge funding. Within days of the close of the 1974–75 financial year, the Community Health Program within the Hospitals and Health Services Commission was identified as being 'flush with funds' and 'eager to take on the refuge funding'. Thus, the Minister for Health approved funding for the eleven refuges, including Nardine, for the three months July to September 1975, with further funding to be granted on an ongoing basis.[65]

Throughout the 1970s and early 1980s, annual grants from the Hospitals and Health Services Commission through the Community

Volunteer worker Mrs Glenis Hunter (right) and two of the mothers who are staying at the Nardine women's refuge.

# Refuge for women has cash crisis

### By Doug Cunningham

The Nardine women's refuge in Mt Lawley is flat broke—almost as destitute as the mothers and children who come knocking at its doors.

The refuge, struggling for funds ever since it opened last July, urgently needs $1500.

Nardine was opened by the Women's Centre Action Group and caters for women and their children who have been forced out of home for various reasons.

The Trades and Labor Council decided this week to start a union fund and back efforts by the refuge for government help.

Four mothers and 17 children are now at the refuge, but up to 30 mothers and 60 children are being turned away each week because there is no room in the three-bedroomed house.

Pat Whitmarsh, one of two workers who run the refuge, said that about $500 a week was needed to keep it going.

"We are expecting some money from the Community Welfare Department but this is going to cover only our debts," she said.

Miss Whitmarsh said the refuge had received a $1000 grant from the Lotteries Commission, which enabled it to buy a washing machine and essential furniture.

"Mothers are asked to pay $2 a night for themselves and $1 a night for each child. This covers food and things like that," she said.

Miss Whitmarsh said there was a desperate need for centres like Nardine. Mothers and children were generally directed there by the Community Welfare Department.

She said that the refuge relied heavily on volunteer help. Many women assisted by the centre in the past often returned to help out.

A mother of two now staying at Nardine said she arrived destitute. She had nowhere to go and was so desperate for money she sold a $120 cassette collection for $10 and other possessions for virtually nothing.

Nardine sought community support regarding its funding shortfall through newspaper articles and, at the same time, drew attention to domestic violence and the work of refuges. *Daily News*, 6 February 1975, p. 3. *Courtesy Doug Cunningham; Battye Library*

Health Program, administered through the State Government's Department of Public Health, were Nardine's major source of funds. The greater financial security provided by the Health Department funds allowed Nardine's feminists to further develop the refuge. However, funding was always subject to the vagaries of the State and Commonwealth political climates, and workers were poorly paid.[66] For example, Maggie Lawson recalled that when she first started working at Nardine in 1976, she was paid $15 for a night shift of sixteen hours.[67] Even with ongoing government funding, other fund-raising events such as women's dances and street appeals continued to be held to supplement the limited financial resources. Later in the 1970s, funding became a major battleground as the conservative State Government withdrew its support.

Throughout these difficulties with funding, the day-to-day practice at the refuge evolved within a developing radical feminist framework.

## DEVELOPING RADICAL FEMINISM

While Nardine had been initiated from the more broad-based women's liberation movement, over time the WCAG and those involved with the refuge increasingly adopted radical feminist perspectives.[68] Radical feminism was a way of explaining women's position in society, where gender, rather than class or other social characteristics, was considered most significant in determining disadvantage. According to Nardine's feminists, these gendered structural inequalities existed because of the patriarchal nature of Australian society; that is, basically men had more power than women did.[69] The notion of patriarchy was central to understandings of feminism at Nardine in these early years, and, working in the area of domestic violence, the evidence of the exercise of male power within the family was very obvious. Structural inequality was also evident to the workers in their day-to-day dealings with the State. Anna Spencer, a former Nardine worker, recalled meeting with government officials and noting

> the gender situation at the time, or rather the lack of gender mix, I suppose…It was obvious, on one side of the table would be all

these bureaucrats, the men in the black suits, and on the other, were the women from the refuge and it was as though we were worlds apart.

While there was an understanding that male power was socially constructed rather than biologically determined, at times the ways that patriarchy was understood were linked to deterministic conceptualizations of men and masculinity. Nardine's feminists recognized the structural inequalities that privileged men and disadvantaged women, but they were also concerned with fixed notions about maleness and masculinity. Michele Kosky explained that

we were strongly committed to a feminist view that the world was run by bad men who were part of the patriarchy and we had no recognition of why domestic violence occurred. We had a very simple idea that women were good and men were bad. That was in the nature of things. That women were fundamentally oppressed by marriage, and that often violence ensued, for a whole range of reasons though we didn't know what they were.

Clearly, there were contradictions in these ideas. Some of the WCAG women were married but at the same time believed that men were inherently 'bad'. Women managed these contradictions in different ways. Kosky commented that husbands were 'silent partners' and that the women 'didn't really talk about the men we were married to in our dealings with the collective. That was a private part of our lives and that we'd unfortunately fallen into the trap of marriage'. But in the early years, these men did some maintenance work for the refuge and had also acted as guarantors for the lease. In the late 1970s, Nardine employed a homosexual male child-care worker and for some time a group of male university students took children out on weekends. The rationale was to ensure that children had access to positive male role models. Thereafter, however, men were no longer employed or taken on as volunteers at the refuge. Despite these earlier attempts to include men, the sense that masculinity was problematic became stronger. Kosky recalled that she would come home from meetings on Monday nights and lie in bed next to her husband, concerned that she was 'sleeping with the enemy'. Others eventually dealt with these contradictions by leaving their male partners. Their decision was aligned with developing radical feminist ideas about changing the nature of relationships as part of the larger transformation of society:

> For radical feminists, women, as women, were oppressed not by capitalism but by patriarchal domination by men. The struggle was therefore to be directed primarily against men and male-dominated culture. 'The personal is political': relationships, language, loving, all had to be revolutionized because they reflected this domination.[70]

Radical feminism was to have dramatic implications for Nardine, as well as for individual women who lived and worked there.

## SISTERHOOD AND DIFFERENCE

One of the underpinning assumptions of radical feminism was the belief that there were significant differences between men and women; that, as Anna Spencer commented, men and women were 'worlds apart'. Another was a notion of sisterhood that relied on the premise that in all instances the commonalities between women overrode the differences produced by other social categories. This was outlined by a Perth radical feminist:

> Recognition by wimin of their oppression in a sexist society and the political struggle against sexism in themselves and in society. Feminists do not deny there are other oppressive forces (economic, racial, educational etc) but see the fight against sexism as the cohesive force needed to unite all wimin in political struggle.[71]

Michele Kosky, for example, recalled that the focus of these commonalities for her at the time were women's experiences of their bodies, marriage and children. Domestic violence itself was understood as an experience shared by women that cut across class, ethnic, racial and other social characteristics. In contrast to more popular views that domestic violence was an experience of working-class women, Nardine's feminists argued that violence affected women of all social categories.

But in the day-to-day life of the refuge, difference was an issue of some significance, and the women involved with Nardine in the early years attempted to work with it. Class was one factor that became an important measure of difference. As wealthier women were much more likely to have access to alternative accommodation, Nardine's residents tended to be drawn from poorer economic backgrounds. In the earliest years, the workers and members of the WCAG were largely from middle-class backgrounds. Kosky explained:

> I had no formal role in the day to day running though I would go over and help, do the dishes, mind children. I didn't talk to women that much because I felt their lives were very different to mine. I didn't think I had much to contribute…[I didn't know] any better how they might make their lives agree to feminist principles when we were all muddling through in ours.

By 1976, class had become a major site of conflict for some Nardine workers and the WCAG, and over a period of time there was decreasing involvement by WCAG women. Residents and former residents were encouraged by some workers to take over the management and staffing of the refuge as a means of self-empowerment, and during the late 1970s the refuge was run largely by a group of residents and former residents.

Race and ethnicity were also social cleavages that were clearly evident among residents and workers. Workers from these early years were largely from Anglo-Australian backgrounds and acknowledged that they had limited understanding of the issues facing Indigenous women and those of non-Anglo backgrounds. However, Nardine provided opportunities for them to work with and learn about cultural differences, and working with Aboriginal women taught them a lot about Indigenous cultures and racism and its effects.

For Indigenous women, even more so than for other women, the wider society offered little support to those experiencing domestic violence. In fact, the two authorities from which some assistance could be sought—the police and 'the welfare'—were those that Indigenous people often profoundly distrusted because of their ongoing impact on their families.[72] In contrast, Nardine offered safe, supportive and non-institutionalized accommodation. Among the refuges in Perth, it 'gained a reputation in the Aboriginal community as being a safe and accepting place for Aboriginal women to go to'.[73] Nardine was the first non-Indigenous managed refuge in Western Australia to implement a policy of affirmative action around employment of Indigenous women, in recognition of the needs of the women and children coming to the refuge.

Routinely, and at any one time, half or more of Nardine's residents have been Indigenous women and their children—a remarkable proportion. Indigenous people make up approximately 3 per cent of Western Australia's population and nearly a third of the total women's refuge population.[74] This suggests that they experience family violence to a greater extent than other women do, or that the effects of this violence on Indigenous women are such that they are more likely to use refuges.

Indigenous women, particularly, felt the impact of social disadvantage and discrimination. One way in which this was manifested was through the difficulties they experienced in gaining housing, and at times they could remain at the refuge for extended periods while waiting for suitable, affordable housing to become available. During the mid-1970s, campaigns were run to raise awareness of Indigenous homelessness, which included those who were homeless as a result of family violence.

A lot of Aboriginal women are without basic shelter. They are living with their children in empty car bodies, on river banks, or with relatives. When they stay with their relatives they overcrowd and bring the risk of eviction onto these relatives too, for being prepared to share what they have with their less fortunate family members.[75]

Even though discrimination against Indigenous women clearly produced experiences substantially different to those of other women, and there was sensitivity to this disadvantage, radical feminism remained the overriding guiding philosophy of the refuge. In more recent years, the severity and extent of violence against Indigenous women and the impact of social disadvantage and racism have been more widely recognized within the domestic violence field.

The establishment of Nardine was a response to domestic violence that was born out of the women's liberation movement and the movement against domestic violence that emerged in the 1970s. Through skilful lobbying, feminists secured ongoing government funding for the service. In addition to the day-to-day work of running the refuge, they also took political action to inform others of the extent and severity of domestic violence and its impact on the lives of women and children affected by it. In doing so, they gave practical expression to the feminist slogan of the times, that 'the personal is political'.

# CHAPTER — 3

# Feminism in action: Philosophy and practice at Nardine

We're talking about an era in history where this hadn't been done before, where women hadn't left or if they had left, they hadn't received any assistance and it was unheard of…the idea of women making their own decisions and being assisted to make their own decisions and encouraged and getting out and saying, 'no, this is enough'…I think it was also empowering for many of the women who made that transfer and actually actively became involved in the running of an organization, which they might never have thought that they could do. I think it was empowering for the workers…It was a time that you felt very much part of something big that was happening, part of a powerful process, a social change process that was occurring.

SUE ALLEN, 1998[1]

Feminism was part of the day-to-day life of Nardine Women's Refuge. It was apparent in the refuge's work in providing women and children with an environment that promoted their empowerment, and in the organization of the refuge as a collective. Both empowerment and collectivity were issues concerning power, and the analysis of power was central to Nardine's feminism. Nardine's feminists came to understand domestic violence as a manifestation of the power inequities that existed within the most personal of relationships between men and women. Refuge workers attempted to provide circumstances in which women who had been disempowered by domestic violence could regain their own power, and, as a group, they attempted to share power through collectivity.

Significantly, and in line with the feminist slogan 'the personal is political', workers also considered the dynamics of power within their own personal relationships. For many, this meant becoming what was known as 'women-identified'—that is, attempting to view the world from feminine perspectives, rather than from understandings based on notions that assumed the masculine to be the norm. More radically, for some, it meant embarking on lesbian relationships. For others who already identified as lesbians, it gave a positive acknowledgment to lesbian sexuality found in few other workplaces.

This chapter discusses how feminist philosophy and practice came together in the early years at Nardine.

## EMPOWERING WOMEN

Nardine's feminists were concerned with individuals and their potential for personal change. Thus, the concept of empowerment of women was central to the work of the refuge. This process was elaborated by the Women's Refuge Group, the peak body of Western Australian refuges, of which Nardine was an active member:

> The primary importance of any refuge is that it provides women and children with a supportive environment. For many women this will be the first time she is encouraged and assisted to recognise her identity and make decisions about her and her children's futures.[2]

It was also recognized that empowerment was about more than personal change for individual women. According to refuge movement feminists, it also had implications for wider social change:

> By providing an environment in which it becomes possible for women to contemplate alternatives and to develop support systems, the refuge plays a significant part in improving the status of all women in society. Not only is this dealt with on a personal level, but just as importantly in the broader social context. That is, the existence of refuges highlights the significant extent of domestic violence despite the public's attempts to ignore the issue and, in turn, refuges (either individually or collectively) attempt to improve the services women receive—be it health, housing, legal or welfare services.[3]

Typically, women came to Nardine feeling disempowered as a result of their experiences of domestic violence. Nardine's goal was to support women to take control of their lives. April Davis, a worker at Nardine in the 1970s, described this process:

> 'If they've been in a situation where they were put down all the time, they start believing what they were told. In some relationships there's no physical violence at all, but the mental violence is atrocious. We've had women in here who haven't been allowed to do their own shopping. The men had to go with them because they didn't trust them with the money. Those women had to ask every time they wanted a packet of cigarettes.
>
> 'They've been told that they were stupid. They've been told that they were ugly. That if they left no man would have them and "where could you go with four kids anyway? You should consider yourself lucky you've got me", etc etc. And they believed.
>
> 'Then they find they do have somewhere to go, and whether there is another male to take them or not isn't important. They can cope by themselves. Even though it would be nice to have another relationship, it is not something you *need*.'[4]

Maggie Lawson described what empowerment meant to her as a resident at Nardine:

> For me personally, it meant that I wasn't the only one in the situation, that there were other people from a range of other backgrounds that were coming from the same situation, that there were things that I could do about it, that I could make a life for myself, without having to have a man in my life. Yes, there was a life after domestic violence. That I could be safe with my children, that I could be safe from this person, and that there were things that could be put in place to make it as safe as possible…Also I learnt about feminism, I learnt about women helping women and that was new to me, to actually support other women, that was not part of what I knew.[5]

The understanding of women's lives through shared experiences was an important aspect of providing an environment supportive of empowerment. Anna Spencer recalled her feelings when she first came to Nardine:

> I had this image of me walking up the path to the main door. I had a two year old on one side and an overbrimming suitcase on the other. I remember tripping over and I actually remember my knee bleeding and just having an awful sort of desolation. I was glad of that image later because it constantly reminded me when new people were coming into the refuge as residents when I was a worker, of how they must have felt.[6]

How, then, did Nardine work with women to provide the circumstances in which they could be empowered? Ensuring women's and children's safety was always workers' first response. As elsewhere where the domestic violence movement developed from the 1970s, the feminist response was to provide refuge. This strategy came out of the prevailing circumstances in which police (and other human service agencies) did not act to protect women and children in their own homes. In many cases, instead of the male perpetrator being removed, women and children left their homes, seeking safety elsewhere. And even if the violent husband was removed, it was usually only temporarily and he would return, leaving women and children potentially vulnerable. In the early years, refuge workers themselves assisted women and children to leave their homes, which could be dangerous and frightening for all involved. However, from the mid-1980s, with the development of the Crisis Care Unit in Western Australia, refuge workers were assisted by others who took on this aspect of crisis intervention work and with some recognition by police of their role in assisting victims of domestic violence.

If women and children came to the refuge from situations of physical violence, an immediate concern was to take them to hospital or a local doctor, to ensure that any physical health issues were addressed. Providing emotional support to women was another immediate and ongoing response, and this helped women to begin to make sense of their situation. Workers were very much a part of the day-to-day lives of the residents; listening was a primary means of providing emotional support. Especially at night, when children had gone to bed, workers spent time just talking with residents. Deborah Dearnley explained that refuge work had involved 'a lot of time sitting with women, listening to their life stories and their experiences of domestic violence'.[7] Most workers were not trained psychologists or social workers but rather women who had understanding of and empathy for others. As Sue Allen recalled, it was 'counselling with a little "c"'. Allen came to work at Nardine at a strikingly young age, given the nature of the work, and, as she acknowledged, 'at 17 or 18, I'm not sure I was particularly skilled'. Others, however, brought considerable skill to their work:

> You'd have various times sitting listening; they'd need to emotionally debrief about what had happened. The emotional side of domestic violence is horrific. Sometimes women would need to go over and over and over what had happened or where they'd been.[8]

At some times during Nardine's history, subject to staffing resources, ongoing emotional support was provided through an outreach service for women after they left the refuge. While those outside the refuge may have thought that spending 'three hours…drinking cups of tea just talking through issues' with former residents was not a legitimate use of workers' time—and, indeed, it was considered by some workers as 'having a bit of a holiday'—Nardine believed that this was an extremely important part of service provision and ongoing support.[9]

The provision of emotional support, although essential, was not without its problems. Particularly during the 1970s and 1980s, relationships in the refuge between workers and residents were based on a friendship model that was anti-professional

> in keeping with feminist roles that, if we were to see ourselves as professionals, we would distance ourselves from the women that

were in the refuge. Breaking down those kind of boundaries was making a statement that in many ways we were no different, we were all equal.[10]

While this model could work well, at times boundaries between workers and residents became blurred, as Glenda Blake recalled: 'you would take women home...give women your home phone numbers, you'd almost kind of live and breathe refuge work, at work and at home'.[11] Similarly, Kedy Kristal noted that Nardine tried to break down the structure of 'I'm the worker, you're the resident', but that while this model had benefits, it 'then became really murky in lots of other ways as well'.[12] In addition, in retrospect, the kind of emotional support provided by some workers encouraged dependency and could thus be considered disempowering. Sue Allen explained:

I can remember it happening where someone started working who needed to be needed or perhaps hadn't resolved their own issues to do with domestic violence or sexual abuse or all sorts of things. They needed to be needed and they needed to help. They may not have been clear with themselves about what that need was about but the consequence is that if that's what's operating in you, then it's important that you do help and it's important that someone is the 'helpee', so you can encourage a dependency. You can end up trying to look after and protect people and in fact reinforce their victim status rather than encouraging people to do for themselves.

Women at the refuge also gained considerable support from each other, as Daphne Smith recalled:

I can remember lots of times women would be sitting around the table...with it being a communal environment...gradually they'd realise that the women who were there weren't down and outers and weirdoes and all sorts of things, that they were like them. And you'd hear them sitting there saying, 'Oh God, these guys must have had a script, my old man used to say that to me.' And it's true…you'd think that they all went to a school of domestic violence to learn how to treat your woman badly. And they learnt so much from each other and sometimes we used to just sit in and help to move them along.[13]

An indication of the level of support among residents in the refuge came through displays of culinary expertise:

I remember a woman who used to make these huge cook-ups and that's one of the recurring themes that I remember about Nardine is that if the house was going particularly well, there'd be these huge cook-ups of these different nationality foods.[14]

Communal living required mutual trust and support. It could be difficult for some, especially as Nardine used a non-institutional model that insisted on the minimum of house rules. In other refuges, there were rules about everything. At Nardine, however, there were 'few rules and much chaos'.[15] The intention was that the refuge be thought of as the women's and children's home, and that they should be able to live there as they would in their own home. This meant, according to Diana Warnock, that there were 'no limits to women's behaviour'.[16] For example, in the earliest years, alcohol was allowed in the refuge, and some women went out with the loosest child-care arrangements, assuming that there would always be someone to look after the children. However, such flexibility and freedom led to tensions between residents' choices and the rights of others. In 1975, the need for rules was discussed:

Whether or not to be home early or to come in at any hour which means waking someone up and then being too tired or hung over to look after kids in the morning.[17]

There was much heated discussion in the collective over a long period of time before, for example, alcohol was banned in the early 1980s.

Today, with greater emphasis on public health issues, it is hard to imagine that a service such as a refuge would allow alcohol consumption, but the greater concern at the time was that women made decisions for themselves.

Even after rules about alcohol use were established, workers recalled the refuge as chaotic. They were unable to take control because of the refuge's commitment to allowing the women to live their own lives. At the same time, workers recognized that giving some women power could be disempowering for others.

By the late 1980s, there was increasing concern with providing skilled psychological and emotional assistance and counselling to women, over and above what could be offered by workers or other residents. Libby Best explained:

> Perhaps from my earliest feminist days I thought the world might change and maybe a couple of times when I was a new worker I thought that talking about that kind of thing [structural issues around gendered power] would change women's lives but I learnt very early on that that's not necessarily the case. There's a huge part of domestic violence that's to do with a person's emotional well being and self esteem and belief in themselves and their childhood and their upbringing.[18]

Best reflected a concern not just with the structural issues and their political effects but also with the very personal, psychological effects of the trauma of domestic violence. For some women, this resulted in serious mental health issues that were not addressed adequately by mental health services.

In more recent years, support services for women have been developed and offered by a range of agencies. These include Nardine's and other refuges' outreach women's groups, and others, not necessarily feminist in their approach, such as those provided by generalist welfare services. Some in the refuge movement believe that women's support services continue to be under-resourced and insufficiently

Karen Lockhart, Nardine's outreach worker, listens to a client. The outreach service provides assistance and support to women in the community experiencing domestic violence. *West Australian*, 7 November 2001, p. 36. *Courtesy* West Australian

accessible. In contrast, counselling services for men, initiated in 1998, while important in assisting in the prevention of domestic violence, are free and available by referral from a government telephone helpline.

In line with developing radical feminist understandings of domestic violence, women at Nardine, from the refuge's inception, were introduced to a feminist structural analysis that attempted to place their experiences within the context of a male-dominated patriarchal society. This analysis was based on the notion that women (as a group) had less power than men (as a group), as demonstrated through men's and women's different positions within society, and that this was a result of the ways in which social structures such as the law, education, the family and the church advantaged men. Within this framework, domestic violence was presented as a manifestation of women's relative powerlessness. Over time, further feminist writing offered more sophisticated analyses, such as the 'cycle of violence' theory and, later, the 'power and control' model.[19] These feminist ideas were presented to women to assist them in making sense of their situation and to help them understand, among other things, that it was not their fault. Working against the attitude of 'victim-blaming' formed a significant part of the work of the refuge. Although deterministic in its approach—that is, asserting that we live in a male-dominated society—these ideas, in a somewhat contradictory manner, attempted to give space to women to take control of their own lives. In practice, this structural analysis was delivered in a range of ways:

> Listening to them, taking them seriously, having a real interest, pointing out to them about the whole dynamics of domestic violence. How they could have the perfect meal on the table every night and the kids in bed and they'll still be bashed. So it was nothing that they were doing, it wasn't their fault, it was about control and men's behaviour. And reassuring women and supporting them…talking to them about managing their own money and their housing and taking control of their children…I think for me, there was all that practical stuff involved, but the trickiest thing for me was trying to assist women or give them information

that gave them a different framework to what they'd been living in. That's the bit about either an intellectual framework about what domestic violence is or a different emotional framework that helps them break free.[20]

Talking about feminist ideas was not always welcomed by the women, for a range of reasons. One was the bad name that feminism had in the wider community at that time. While women were willing to use feminist services, they were not necessarily interested in listening to the underpinning philosophies, nor did they have the capacity to understand them, no matter how helpful they might have been. As Daphne Smith pointed out, for some women, feminism and its language were alienating. For others, a feminist structural analysis did not make much sense at a personal level. Hence, feminist ideas were often merely translated into the belief that women were not at fault, that no one had to put up with being mistreated, and that women were strong and could survive.

In the early years, Nardine's workers typically understood that part of women's empowerment came with leaving their violent partners, and residents were actively encouraged to do this. Later, workers recognized that this decision had to be made by the women themselves. Through being provided with information and advocacy on independent income support, housing and related legal issues, women were able to make an informed choice about whether to leave a violent relationship. Both Michele Kosky and Susie Strong, who worked at the refuge in the earliest years, expressed concern retrospectively about not having respected women's autonomy.[21] However, documents from the time (and since) clearly indicated their intention to allow women to make their own decisions:

The workers, both voluntary and paid, at the house aim to offer support and a friendly atmosphere while the people are in residence. Some women who have stayed at the house have returned to their husbands, so it is not the function of the house to separate families but rather to give women the chance to think through their problems and discuss with other people the ramifications of their decisions.[22]

Many women did return to their partners—and, given the options available to women and children in the 1970s, it is not surprising that they did, although some returned to Nardine on later occasions. For example, in statistics collected by the refuge for the period September 1974 to April 1975, it was noted that twenty-one women were rehoused by the State Housing Commission, twenty-two obtained private accommodation, and sixteen were 'reconciled with husband or de facto'.[23]

In retrospect, there was ambivalence about feminism as a form of 'ideological indoctrination'. Michele Kosky reflected that 'women who are subject to domestic violence always pay a price for safety…religious indoctrination or some feminist indoctrination'. While Nardine provided a safe and secure environment for women and children escaping domestic violence and gave them opportunities to reflect upon their lives, workers attempted to influence them by the ideological positions of the WCAG, regardless of the realities of their lives. Women were advised not to return to their violent partners, as they would be better off without them; in hindsight, Kosky acknowledged that indeed perhaps many of the women would not have been. Susie Strong also expressed concern about the options available to women leaving abusive relationships at this time and her part in encouraging them to do so:

Because in those days Lockridge was just ghastly and all the single mums were being shoved out there. Women would come to the refuge and say that men would just go knocking on their doors on Saturday night looking for a fuck. And there were attempted suicides every month. So it was pretty depressing. And I used to feel really depressed that women would come [to the refuge], leave a violent marriage, but their options…You could understand why they went back in some ways because their other options were to go out and live at bloody Lockridge in these cement cells totally isolated. Public transport was lousy. No money, you know, you're reliant on the Salvos or somebody to give you a bit of furniture and a fridge. No wonder most of them went home again and back to their husbands.[24]

Despite the concerns expressed by Kosky and Strong, some women who left their partners tell stories of survival and empowerment. After leaving her husband, Maggie Lawson stayed at Nardine for a month and then moved to a flat where her neighbours included other single mothers. She recalled that this group of women 'all looked after each other' and have remained friends ever since. Lawson had carefully planned leaving her husband, with the support and assistance of Nardine workers. She had left him once before, but he had tracked her down and she was fearful that this would happen again. For her, the decision to leave had led, she believed, to a better life for her and her children.

But there were other concerns with the feminist approach. For example, some workers questioned the capacity of these kinds of models, whether structural or psychological, to account for Indigenous women's experiences of family violence, or their ability to offer any assistance. In recent years, Indigenous responses to family violence have been developed, including healing centres that take a holistic family approach.

Whether women were ever actually 'indoctrinated' by feminism at Nardine, or whether the brand of feminism that was espoused even touched them, is hard to know, but for some—even those who returned to violent partners—some change may have occurred. Libby Best elaborated on the possibilities:

> Empowerment is such a tricky thing too. A woman might come to the refuge and then go back to the same relationship, nothing's changed…There was a whole group of women, sometimes you'd think that coming to the refuge was like a respite from the violence [for them]. To me then empowerment becomes those minute things. Is it longer this time? Is this next relationship not quite as violent? Or do they get out before the violence happens?

As well as ensuring their physical safety and providing emotional support and a framework in which to attempt to understand their experiences, the refuge offered residents practical support. This could be in the form of information about income support, legal issues or housing, or it could be through accompanying women and providing advocacy at interviews and meetings with government departments where they sought financial assistance, housing and other welfare services. In the 1970s, gaining permission to accompany women to such meetings was a battle. Maggie Lawson recollected that government officials insisted that women be interviewed alone. However, Nardine demanded that workers be present to provide support and advocacy where necessary, and this did happen in many instances. Today, having a supporter or advocate present in meetings with government officials is an unquestioned right.

Despite the support and information provided by Nardine's workers to assist in women's empowerment, residents still struggled with the attitudes and practices prevailing in the wider society, particularly in the earlier years of the refuge, when there was little sympathy for victims of domestic violence. For example, Glenda Blake recalled occasions during the early 1980s when women were provided with legal information but then went into court and were denied restraining orders; they were thus disempowered by a system that had little regard for the disadvantage they experienced as women.

Although the Single Mothers' Benefit had been introduced in 1972, the assessment for this government support was stringent, particularly during the 1970s, and women did not automatically receive financial assistance. Women who had left their marital home had to establish their legitimacy as 'deserving' welfare recipients. Maggie Lawson recalled that separated women were required to answer questions about the state of their marital relationship, to show proof that they had left, and to demonstrate that they were taking legal action to separate and to gain custody of their children. Lawson noted that when she had left her husband, she did not know that she was eligible to receive financial support from the government, nor would she have known how to go about obtaining it. The assistance, then, of refuge workers was invaluable in supporting her through this crisis. According to the *Australian Women's Weekly*, in a 1976 article outlining the work of Elsie Women's Refuge, eligible separated women could receive emergency assistance of $47 per week from the New South Wales Department of Youth and Community Services (and similarly from the Department for Community Welfare in Western Australia) and then, after six months, $52 per week in the form of either the Deserted Wives' or the Single Mothers' Benefits.[25]

Residents were also supported to move to independent accommodation. However, refuges have always worked with limited resources, particularly in relation to housing. Michele Kosky remembered the abject poverty of some of the residents who moved from the refuge to long-term accommodation provided by the State Housing Commission in the mid-1970s. She recalled taking a woman and her two children from Nardine to a flat in Fremantle. As the flat was empty and the woman had no furniture, bedding or other resources, Kosky drove back to her own home and returned with food, pillows and blankets. Ensuring that women have access to decent and affordable housing has continued as an important political issue for refuges.

Another way in which the empowerment of residents was promoted was by offering them work at the refuge, particularly during the early years. Indeed, for several years in the late 1970s, the staff of the service largely comprised former residents. The underpinning philosophy was that women, having suffered violence themselves, could use their experiences to the benefit of others. They could

> see that as a valuable experience. Their own journeys in escaping abusive partners had taught these women how to be survivors and they drew on this experience to assist other women in the refuge...It was in keeping with the philosophy...of valuing women's unique experiences rather than positioning ourselves as the 'experts'.[26]

The recognition of their skills and knowledge through the offer of employment at the refuge also challenged feelings of worthlessness instilled through violent relationships. Maggie Lawson remembered the boost that it was to work first as a volunteer and then later, as funding became available, as a paid worker.

## SUPPORTING CHILDREN

> I remember the kids. You'd go into the office to try to do some work and there'd be kids swarming all over you all the time, wanting to be in there. One of the things I remember is the neediness of the kids…because their lives had been disrupted, often the kids were really, really needy kids and of course some of them were really disturbed kids.[27]

Libby Best's memories draw attention to the needs of children, who always make up the majority (approximately two-thirds) of clients in refuges accommodating families.

Children have been the under-resourced clients of refuges. While their presence has been obvious, as the quote above testifies, their needs have often barely been addressed. Children are the most powerless members of families and, like their mothers, must also make sense of their experiences of violence and leaving home. They come to refuges always having witnessed domestic violence and not uncommonly having experienced it directly. Strangely, though, it has been thought by some that children are unaffected by it, or that special services to assist those who are affected are unnecessary.[28] The 1987 report of the evaluation of women's refuges in Western Australia presented compelling evidence of the needs of children in refuges; it recommended that child-care staffing in refuges be increased, that facilities for children in refuges be improved, and that the special needs of Aboriginal children and children from non-English-speaking backgrounds be addressed.[29] However, the development of specific counselling services for children in refuges that attempt to deal with their psychological trauma and distress did not occur until as recently as 1998. Nardine has made extensive use of this service and has found it to be extremely beneficial for children in the refuge, who are often severely traumatized. In earlier years, the funding bodies provided salary subsidies for dedicated child-care workers, but their role was to provide play activities, not to engage directly with emotional and psychological issues.

Nardine has a history of recognizing the presence of children and their relative powerlessness, and of attempting to address their needs through practical support and activities. For all of the refuge's existence, child support or child-care has been part of the work of the refuge, to give women greater freedom to attend appointments and to have their own rest time, but also in recognition of the needs of the children themselves. Child-care workers were responsible for developing and providing children's programs in the refuge, and worked with mothers to address the practical needs of their children. But in earlier years, before service standards set a limit on the number of families who could be accommodated at refuges, child support meant working with large numbers of distressed children of varying ages. It was reported during 1981 that

> [t]here are currently 30 children [at Nardine], including five teenage boys and three teenage girls, all of whom have their own problems associated with violent and stressful homes.[30]

And these thirty children would probably also have included newborn babies, toddlers, preschoolers and primary school age children—all with important and varied needs. (With the introduction of service standards and the maximum number of five families at Nardine in the purpose-built dwelling, it is rare that there would be more than a dozen children resident at any one time now.) Despite the challenges of large numbers of children, there was always a commitment to them, as Glenda Blake recalled:

> There always seemed to be a real emphasis on the children. And I think Nardine was really innovative in that respect because there was always a worker or a couple of workers who insisted that two thirds of the population of the refuge were children and therefore the refuge needed to have a real focus on children whether that be

through very skilled, very child-focused child care workers, or child support workers. And an insistence that all refuge workers needed to respond at different points of the day to the needs of kids.

This commitment to children was manifested in a range of ways over the years. In an early submission for funding, the services offered by Nardine were said to include 'child minding'. However, although children's specific needs were recognized, little could be done: 'our newly appointed part timer is quite unable to meet all the demands of an average of 14 children, most of whom suffer some emotional disturbance, and a number with severe emotional disturbance'.[31] Michele Kosky, on reflection, confirmed these concerns. It is important to recognize the lack of resources and understanding of the issues at this time, in the mid-1970s:

> I don't think we dealt with the children well…We didn't understand that there are behaviours that are unacceptable between mothers and children. Often the mothers came very traumatised from the violence they'd experienced and perpetuated it.

How, then, were children supported? Women coming to the refuge were advised that they would receive some help with their children from refuge workers:

> Your smaller children would be looked after during the day in a well-equipped pre-school, while the older ones went to a nearby school. Several nights a week a refuge worker would help the children with their homework or any other problems, and on weekends she would bundle them into the Nadine [sic] bus for an outing to the movies, the beach, or into the country.[32]

But, as indicated, there was some understanding that children who had come from the highly traumatizing circumstances of domestic violence could need much more than a swim and a hand with their homework.

A job description from 1986 included the requirement that workers 'communicate with and support young people', and they would do this, at least partly, through helping them 'to understand their oppression and lack of rights'. Like their mothers' introduction to feminist understandings of domestic violence and the structural reasons for their oppression, children were also introduced to the politics of power.[33]

Cath Munro, a child-care worker in the early 1980s, recalled the outings and play time with the children. As the mothers were sometimes also present, these occasions provided another opportunity for support:

> Nardine [at Vincent Street] had a big side garden with a big Chinese pepper tree and so lots of the kids would cycle round and round and round and round the tree. So we sat outside a lot with the women and the kids…We would sit out there and talk with the women and watch the kids.

Some of this support came from an understanding of the invisible work that women did for their children:

> I think women carry a lot, contain a lot for their children and often that's silent work. I think coming into the refuge and having that person [the refuge worker] being very interested in their children and what's happening there is very significant in their lives.[34]

Linda Digby, a child support worker at Nardine during the early 1990s, supported children by being 'emotionally available' to them:

> Nothing else seemed to matter if it meant just sort of sitting and talking and being really flexible about what went on in a day's work…painting and…art therapy stuff and just depending on what kids wanted to do at the time…long walks…We spent a lot of time at Kings Park or going swimming or down the beach…story telling…lots of stories in books. That was always

quite a good thing about the child care at Nardine: if you had the opportunity just to have one on one, it was fantastic. And we tried to do that when we could. It wasn't always possible. A range of different things would take place and each day would be quite different.[35]

Sometimes, child-care workers visited schools where refuge children were attending in an attempt to resolve problems raised through disruption and distress. In doing this, the workers spoke to teachers and principals about domestic violence; for some school staff, this was their first contact with refuges and feminist understandings of domestic violence and its impact on children.[36]

Over the years, there have been tragedies involving children at Nardine, and workers recalled their sadness and despair over child deaths. A fire at the refuge claimed the life of a child in the 1980s; another child was hit by a car on Vincent Street. In the earliest years, there was a cot death at Nardine, and a child who returned for a weekend to the home of his mother's violent partner died after being physically assaulted. Each of these children touched the lives of workers at Nardine, and their memories have stayed with them.

## COLLECTIVITY

Until 1997, Nardine operated as a collective. Over the years, the collective structure and its practices varied considerably, but throughout there was a philosophical commitment to shared power and work. Although the collective structure had both its supporters and its critics, workers who were involved with the collective overwhelmingly acknowledged the benefits that they had accrued through working from within this framework. Whether residents gained as much is difficult to assess.

First, though, it is important to outline the nature of collectives, as they are quickly disappearing from the organizational landscape as hierarchical management models take over. Australian social work academic Wendy Weeks explains how non-hierarchical collectivity has been a key organizational principle of feminist women's services. It has been enacted in a range of ways, from shared authority and leadership, consensus decision-making, a division of labour on a shared or rotating basis and salary sharing, through to the total organizational form of the collective. The collective model has been a serious attempt to 'implement democracy' in the workplace.[37] Nardine, for most of its history, provides a case study for each of these processes, as well as an example of the ways that non-conventional structures such as feminist collectives create tensions for government funding bodies.[38]

A commitment to collectivity was evident from Nardine's inception. In 1974, the refuge was initiated and developed under the auspices of the WCAG. At least partly to assist in securing funding from both the State and Commonwealth governments, the WCAG became an incorporated association. While a formalized group, the organization worked collectively, without rigid structures or an obvious hierarchy, in line with feminist principles that challenged notions of the centralization of power and encouraged participation in decision-making. Despite these attempts to challenge existing structures, accountability and incorporation required that there were people in designated positions. Michele Kosky, for example, held the position of secretary to the WCAG in these early years, while the position of chair was rotated from meeting to meeting.

During these early years, the collective was open—that is, anyone with an interest in Nardine, both residents and workers, as well as others virtually 'off the street', could participate in decision-making processes. In the planning stages there were five women, but this had grown to about forty by the time Nardine opened its doors. Soon there were many more with an interest in the project, and meetings were held regularly. As described by Diana Warnock, more than a hundred women would gather at these meetings and attempt to make consensus decisions. It was, she recalled, 'chaotic!'. Despite the chaos, decisions were made on a range of issues including how the refuge would be run, funding sources and applications, and feminist activism in relation to domestic violence.

In hindsight, this unrestrained form of the open collective seems an unwieldy and virtually unworkable structure, but it assisted in making visible the workings of the refuge. It also ensured that the refuge received input and support from those external to the day-to-day workings of the service. In the late 1970s, when former residents were encouraged to become workers at the refuge, the collective became narrowed to residents and workers, some of whom were making the transition from one role to the other. By 1980, the collective was no longer open but comprised exclusively workers, although the number of staff was as high as twenty, with the sharing of eight full-time salary subsidies (later reduced through funding cuts to 6.5). From around this time, former residents were no longer the main source of workers.

The workers' collective both delivered services and managed the agency. Among other matters, the workers were responsible for recruiting new staff, managing each other's performance (at least in theory) and, where necessary, discipline and dismissal. Accountability to funding bodies was the responsibility of the collective, and the contact person at any particular time could be one of a number of workers—much to the frustration of departmental officers; recently, as is more common with community-based organizations, the contact person has been the chairperson of the management committee or the coordinator. In earlier times, there was also the sense that Nardine was accountable to the women's movement. However, there were no formal processes in place, only informal understandings that Perth's feminists had an interest in Nardine and were aware through women's networks of the work Nardine was doing and of how, as an organization, it was faring. After all, a considerable number of Perth feminists had at one stage or another either worked at Nardine or, in the earliest days, been volunteers there. By the late 1980s, the number of workers had decreased as individuals chose to take up full-time work, and the closed collective that did the work and managed the organization comprised as few as six women.

In the mid-1990s, the conservative Liberal Party Minister for Family and Children's Services, Roger Nicholls, with little empathy for the community services sector, finally gave Nardine an ultimatum: if Nardine (and other collectives within the sector) did not change to a management committee structure, it would cease to be funded.[39] Threats of loss of funding had been used before, and resistance had won on every previous occasion, but this time the refuge was unsuccessful. Even though the minister was unsympathetic, public servants within his department worked with considerable understanding and expertise to assist Nardine to move towards a new structure.

The change to a management committee structure in 1997 and the employment of the first designated hierarchical position of coordinator in 1998 were not unproblematic for Nardine. The management structure is a challenge to Nardine's long-held philosophical position about power sharing through consensus decision-making and shared work, leadership and payment. Workers who survived the transition felt it hardest. However, elected management committee members, who have included former residents, former workers and other feminists, retain a commitment to participatory democracy and consultation. Strategies that have attempted to minimize the impact of the

Gathering of Nardine staff and management committee, December 2000.
*Courtesy Suellen Murray*
*Front row (left to right):* Louise Langhorn, Elke Kaiser, Tina Fernandes, Kelley Molloy, Allessandra Traverso *Middle row:* Elenie Kolitsis, Lou Kyle, Nova McCormack, Anna Brown, Dawn Bessarab, Jackie Corby, Rahimah Abdullah, Lois Gatley *Back row:* Suellen Murray, Faduma Ahmed Hassan, Eversley Ruth, Deborah Dearnley

centralization of power include the existence of a 'broader collective', or membership, and workers' representation on the management committee. On the positive side, the management committee structure has ensured the increased openness of the refuge's operations and allowed for greater external input to the organization—that is, the refuge has been able to draw on a wider range of expertise, which was formerly available only from the small pool of workers. It has also allowed for management responsibilities to be taken from the workload of workers so that there is more time for service delivery.

How, then, did the collective work in practice? It operated on a commitment to sharing work, with decision-making by a consensus process that assumed that all information was shared. Work was divided in different ways at different times. In the early years, all workers did everything, with individuals nominating themselves to take on particular tasks. This system required commitment, self-responsibility, self-discipline and maturity. Later, specific duties were identified, such as administration, advocacy and support work with the residents, child-care and outreach, and duties were rotated among workers for periods of three months. (One exception, at times, was child-care, where workers were employed specifically for those duties.) But even with increased clarity around tasks, considerable initiative and responsibility were required. There was never a 'boss', and no worker had the job of (formally) telling others what to do. There was also no formal process of supervision or support of workers, nor routine shift handover (except for the refuge day book, which records much of Nardine's life), nor induction for new workers—all roles commonly undertaken by a coordinator in a small service such as Nardine.

Sharing information, giving people space to voice their opinions and the development of a team were strategies implemented at Nardine with the aim of sharing power, but these were not unproblematic. The collective had to meet frequently to ensure that all workers knew what was going on, as there was no central person (such as a coordinator) who held key information. In the early years, the collective would meet one evening during the week, in the workers' personal, unpaid time. Later, workers were paid to attend collective meetings. These meetings were notoriously long and arduous. Consensus decision-making meant that every worker had a say:

> My first experience of sitting within the collective, the first meeting, was everyone going round and having their voices heard. And I thought, 'oh no, if I say something, no one's going to listen to me'. And that must have been my experience from other workplaces where, yes, you may give your opinion but it's not going to be heard or it's not going to be respected. But I really didn't feel that in the collective…And that had a fairly lasting impact, that I can have something to say.[40]

This consensus approach also required that everyone agreed with, or at least that no one objected to, decisions being made. One person disagreeing could result in the status quo remaining. Kedy Kristal recalled feeling 'absolutely gobsmacked' at the power of one person to say 'no' against the wishes of the majority of the collective, and at times this occurred.

For the collective to work well, there had to be a strong team. For Anna Spencer, the members provided support to each other:

> I suppose it was my first involvement in a team environment where there was group thinking, group decision making, consensus, all those sorts of things; that was really interesting. I found that it was also very powerful for developing confidence. The group protected each other, it promoted self awareness, it encouraged participation and for many women they really felt as though they were being heard for the very first time. That was the power of the group, the support and the encouragement that was happening. I remember that we always referred to each other as sisters and that was a term that was all about mutual respect and caring, caring and sharing. We did share a lot of experiences together.

At other times, there were splits in the collective along friendship or relationship lines, or along ideological lines. These tensions could be 'very strong and very obvious', as Kedy Kristal recalled, sometimes manifesting at collective meetings where 'we all sat on this side and they sat on that side'. The lack of boundaries also lent itself to problematic working relationships within the collective. Glenda Blake has vivid memories of

> some awful altercations with some workers…to do with the fact that there were no boundaries around the workplace. And there was a group of women with very different ideas about what refuge work was about and how you worked with women and children, how you related to other workers…we had workers at the time who were in relationships with each other and there were some very difficult issues that arose around that.

The working of the collective as a team was demonstrated in a range of ways. One way was through the policy that interviews for new workers would be undertaken by all collective members. In the early 1980s, this meant that applicants could be interviewed by up to a dozen women. Some, including Glenda Blake, found this process 'incredibly daunting'. In retrospect, it might seem that collective interviewing was an inappropriate use of workers' time and that the task of selecting a new worker should have been delegated to a smaller team. However, the collective took the view that it was important for all workers to have a say in the employment of new staff.

For new workers, being interviewed prior to commencement was only the first hurdle. After a suitable period of time, as indicated in a job advertisement from the 1980s, they would be 'assessed' for their suitability to work at Nardine:

> Nardine Wimmin's Refuge requires a worker. This [sic] will be a six week training/assessment period during which time you will get to know the collective and about the refuge. At the end of this time we decide whether or not you join the collective.[41]

The assessment of new workers was also undertaken by all members of the collective, and this process, like the interview, could be difficult.

Nardine regularly evaluated its service, and during these events

> some workers regarded that as a time that we would honestly evaluate our work performance and each other's work performance and feel quite safe to share with each other what we despised about each other…I can remember workers leaving the room with tears running down their face…I can remember…starting to smoke again when I had given up…but I've since discovered that's what evaluations are about wherever you go [among community organizations]. Blood letting.[42]

Others took a more pragmatic view:

> I have memories of workers being able to say the most confronting things to me that in another workplace you would be protected from…we did incredibly well despite all that and did manage to support each other. Sometimes we were cruel to each other. But I suppose out of the collective model or out of our sense of feminism there was always someone to support you.[43]

Although the collective professed to share power, and at times attempts were made to subvert the centralization of power, inevitably some collective members were more powerful than others. For example, Joan Groves noted her experience of working in an environment where she did not know the rules and there were no policies in place to help her. In other words, power was not shared with her:

> There seemed to be an agenda running…I never quite knew what it was or what the rules were or how to belong to this group whose ideology became the dominating ideology…I found it all so confusing, to nut it out and to try to understand the dominating ideology that was never actually verbalised.[44]

Others acknowledged that they were part of a group that held greater power. The exercise of power could be very evident in decision-making processes:

We used to have to reach a consensus which just means as far as I can see that the persons with the most powerful personalities at that time or the most influence end up pushing the issue to the extent that people give up even if they don't agree. So I think there was in fact a very clear hierarchy. It's just that it wasn't a formal hierarchy which had some problems because when it's not a formal hierarchy you can't challenge it formally because it doesn't exist anyway.[45]

Another aspect of power sharing was around skills development across the collective of workers. For some, the collective provided opportunities for skills development:

I didn't go in there just to work with the women but I was able to involve myself in all other aspects of the refuge such as the Women's Refuge Group…It gave me that opportunity to do the things that coordinators do but I wasn't paid for it…It gave me group work skills and taught me a lot about working in a team and fostering a team environment.[46]

Some workers, according to Cath Munro, 'blossomed' under the collective structure; at other times, however, the collective became 'immobilized'. The lack of skills of some workers, as defined by the collective of the day, was at times highly problematic and on one occasion led to a controversial discontinuation of employment and an unfair dismissal claim. While, theoretically, the collective professed to share skills and promote skills development, this was very difficult in practice, given the work conditions. However, the need for skills development was not unique to Nardine. In her 1987 evaluation of women's refuges, Ludo McFerran reported that only a third of Western Australian refuge workers believed that they were sufficiently trained to do their job, and 85 per cent of all workers wanted further training.[47] At Nardine, increasingly, it was recognized that all workers did not have equal skills, even with the potential of skills development, but rather that each worker had her own particular strengths, which could be maximized.

In more recent times, particularly in response to the introduction of the first industrial award for Western Australian refuge workers, the Crisis Assistance, Supported Housing (CASH) Award, in 1998, there has been increasing professionalization of workers, with new workers having to meet minimum experience and qualifications criteria. The implementation of performance management is another contemporary tool that has assisted workers to identify areas of skills development and training needs.

A major concern for some about the collective in its latter years was its internal focus and capacity for self-reflection, which could occur at the expense of client services. From the earliest days of the collective, Sue Allen recalled the meetings and their seeming interminability: 'I can remember we would sit there for hours and hours like through till early hours in the morning. It would take all day to go through'. Glenda Blake remarked that 'some of it was incredibly frustrating. I remember arguing, seemingly endlessly, about issues and feeling like you never ever came to any resolution'. These processes, at times, lent themselves to greater focus on the organization than on service delivery.

The nature of the collective and individual responsibility also contributed to an inability to undertake long-term planning:

> Sometimes it was very difficult to make one person responsible for something in particular so it was easy for things not to get done…Because we were always under threat from being a collective it was hard to be visionary in what you did because you felt you were always protecting your turf in a way.[48]

For all that, though, individuals like Deborah Dearnley, the inaugural coordinator of Nardine and a worker there in the late 1970s, continue to be committed to the collective model, where 'every individual makes a commitment to examining, discussing and challenging their own personal philosophies and considering new ways of doing things'. For Dearnley (and for many others), the collective 'taught me a great deal about myself and about working with women and about the practice of feminism, and that was an invaluable experience'.

## WOMEN-IDENTIFIED WOMEN, LESBIANISM AND RADICAL FEMINISM

'The personal is political' was a philosophical underpinning that was translated not only into the day-to-day work practices with women and children and in the running of the organization, but also, for some women, into life-changing experiences. An aspect of radical feminism was its focus on the affirmation of femaleness, and this had practical application in the work of the refuge and in the lives of both residents and workers. Empowerment was partly concerned with improving the self-worth of residents through emphasizing their worth as female human beings. For example, Glenda Blake recalled that there was a real focus on what women could achieve and what women should be able to do that went far beyond domestic violence. Part of this process was valuing women and their experiences, and so, as Linda Digby recollected, Nardine strove to make the time to hear women, to let women talk and to be emotionally available to them and to their children. This was a significant change in approach. To take a woman's perspective in a male-dominated world was to challenge some of the most taken-for-granted assumptions about how people's lives were understood. As Gisela Kaplan reminds us:

> [B]efore 1968 'woman' did not exist as a political category. There were no special services for women, and in almost no area in public life, in scholarship or government were women named and included as a group with rights…Women had to create the category 'woman' themselves and also claim special rights and interests.[49]

Nardine's feminists were among those who actively participated in creating the category 'woman' and claimed her rights and interests through the process of 'women-identification'. This involved taking a woman's point of view, and challenging stereotypical ideas about femininity. For some, it was also about creating a women-only subculture that was born out of lesbian separatist politics. Critiques of the concept of 'woman' have since highlighted the problematic nature of such goals, but, to their credit, there was at the time some recognition among Nardine's feminists of the diversity of who these 'women' could be and of their range of interests and rights.

There were contradictions in Nardine's goals of taking women's point of view as well as confronting dominant understandings of femininity. On the one hand, workers strove to provide a good service through listening and being emotionally available; on the other, they had to learn to set limits. Always saying 'yes', a traditional feminine trait, had to be confronted. Glenda Blake, among others who worked at Nardine, recollected having

> to learn things like saying 'no' to women. And being called the most atrocious names when you said no and becoming confident with that. I mean, you could go to a hundred assertiveness training courses but nothing would have given me a sense of assertiveness like my work at Nardine.

Saying 'no' was part of learning to take care of themselves as workers—again, a challenge to feminine learning about making others' care their first priority. The difficult and stressful work in the refuge forced workers to think about their own self-care. Workers could become caught up in violent and frightening situations:

> I remember going around to houses, [you'd] make sure the bloke wasn't there, get the woman's belongings and stuff. I got caught there once with a woman going back; he came back, which was quite horrific. Took us an hour to get away and when we did he smashed all the windows in the house, tried to smash the van.[50]

Women-identification also challenged ideas about what women should look like. As Glenda Blake explained, among refuge workers in the 1980s, many of whom worked for politically conservative local councils and religious organizations, Nardine's workers were the 'ones who always looked different. The Nardine workers always stood out. They were the overall days and the spiky hair cuts'. Short hair and

Radical feminists were in the news in the 1980s, including through their involvement in women's peace camps protesting against all forms of violence. Typically they were represented as tough and 'unfeminine', as indicated by this Bill Mitchell cartoon concerned with the Sound Women's Peace Camp held at Point Peron in Western Australia in 1984. *Sunday Times*, 9 December 1984, p. 7.
*Courtesy Rhonda Mitchell; Battye Library*

overalls were a uniform worn by many feminist refuge workers that questioned other forms of feminine appearance and attire at the time. 'Hairy-legged lesbians' was a phrase often thrown at women who worked in feminist refuges. Radical feminists' appearance, and their politics, were caricatured in cartoons such as that by Bill Mitchell depicting feminists' engagement with the police at the Sound Women's Peace Camp held south of Perth in 1984 (see above).

In a further strategy to challenge masculine perspectives, in 1987 Nardine changed its name to Nardine Wimmin's Refuge. All constitutional references to 'woman' and 'women' were altered to 'wimmin' and, in refuge correspondence, this spelling was routinely used. These changes did not go unnoticed. In an opinion column in the *West Australian*, Tim Atkinson asked, 'Has Australian society honestly reached the stage where terrified females and children seeking urgent help at a government funded centre must pay heed to radical feminist politics?'.[51] Indeed it had, and, unbeknown to Atkinson and others, radical feminism had been informing responses to domestic violence for some time.

Radical feminism had further personal implications at Nardine. From the earliest years, the radicalization of the WCAG and those involved with Nardine was starkly evident in their changing personal and sexual relationships. From 1975, some women became increasingly concerned with the issue of sexuality. Opportunities for formal discussion routinely occurred prior to the regular Monday night meetings. Susie Strong recalled that information was arriving in Perth from the United States and the Eastern States of Australia about the feminist politics of lesbianism; this was new territory for Perth women. Strong recalled attending these meetings and then becoming

> absolutely scared, terrified, so I stopped going to them for a while but everybody else kept going. I felt left out, so I went back. And then that's when we all started leaving husbands and boyfriends and running off with other women.

Some of the workers from this period played out their radical feminism on personal levels through lesbian relationships, further enacting feminism's famous 1970s slogan 'the personal is political'. In addition to the changing political understandings of sexuality, as historian Kerreen Reiger has noted in relation to mothers' organizations, working closely together 'generated new and intense friendships, which for some, at least, became sexual'.[52] These changes in understandings of women's sexuality had an impact on both workers and residents. Lesbian relationships challenged social norms about women's sexuality and their emotional and economic bonds with men.

Anna Spencer recalled the experience of coming into the refuge in the mid-1970s and making sense, firstly, of feminism:

> I suppose the feminism that was being pushed at the time was coming from the originating group, the Women's Centre Action

Group, and it was very, very confusing for people like myself, coming into the refuge firstly as a resident, because I didn't have the background, I didn't understand what the women's movement was doing at the time. I was like a lot of women who were just concentrating on their young children. That just about took up their whole existence. And if you didn't have the links, if you weren't in a particular group that knew what was going on, you were quite isolated, so I found that the feminism that was happening at the time was quite confusing to come to grips with.

Part of the feminism evident at Nardine at this time was concerned with women's sexuality, as Spencer explained further:

There was definitely an element of lesbianism that was happening at the time. And it was quite confusing to work out how much influence the lesbians in the Women's Centre Action Group had over what was actually happening. For example, women were being very affectionate to each other and obviously there were some lesbian relationships…And there was also a lot of affection being shown which could have been misleading so people had to work out, what is really happening here and what does this brand of feminism mean?…I probably thought as a lot of people did when they first had contact, 'what is going on here?' Something so new and so different and it really was a case of trying to work it out. I think probably my first impression was like 'I'll be here as long as I have to be and then that will be it'. Whereas it wasn't too long down the track when I really wanted to be a part of it. I started to understand what was really happening. And to put things in to some sort of perspective. But group living in itself is quite alien to what most of us know, we're not brought up in that type of environment so that in itself was something very different and I guess it was a case of making allowances because you needed to be there anyway. While you were making those allowances you were starting to open up and be a bit more receptive and to learn what was happening and start questioning and getting some sort of understanding and appreciation of what was going on at the time.

While some, like Spencer, were able to make sense of radical feminist politics, and others were probably untouched by the sexual involvements of the workers, there were those who were not impressed:

> The Aboriginal [workers] were heterosexual, as I was. The dominating ideology was lesbian…they had a really strong subculture and they lived and moved within the subculture whereas the rest of us didn't. We went home, that was it. We only had our stuff at the refuge…It certainly raised questions of discomfort in my mind on a number of occasions in that I thought that if we stood around talking about male partners…would that have been as acceptable? I think not.[53]

Not surprisingly, the highly intense relationships and the blurring between private and working lives led to tensions.

Throughout Nardine's history, lesbian workers have been employed at the refuge. Refuge employment policy continues to encourage the hiring of lesbians (as well as Indigenous women and women of culturally and linguistically diverse backgrounds) in recognition of the discrimination experienced by them (sexuality was not included as grounds for discrimination when the Western Australian *Equal Opportunity Act* was passed in 1984) and in acknowledgment of the contribution made by lesbians to the history of the refuge. Again, taking such a stance did not go unnoticed. In 1989, Nardine advertised for a worker and identified lesbians, among others, as preferred workers. Not only did this result in damning letters to newspapers, including from the anti-feminist Confraternity of Men, but it also resulted in Nardine's workers getting a rap over the knuckles from the funding body: 'lesbian' was a dirty word not to be used in relation to those services so desperately trying to look like they did not break up families. In earlier times, though, the funding body had been more supportive about accusations of 'lesbianism'. Cath Munro recalled an incident when graffiti written on the very exposed refuge fence on Vincent Street proclaimed the workers' assumed sexuality. When informed of this, the funding body was unconcerned.

While there were tensions around making sexuality visible, for some women at Nardine, both workers and residents, exposure to the understanding that sexuality was socially constructed within a world that promoted 'compulsory heterosexuality' and the ensuing masculine advantage led to significant life changes.[54] And the politicization of the personal had ramifications beyond sexuality for workers as they considered the impact of a patriarchal society on family, education, work and other areas of their lives. Susie Strong noted that while the residents were becoming empowered, her life was also changing:

> In a sense I probably was doing it for myself as well, this taking some control of your life. I think that once I became involved with feminism, I looked back at the choices in my life and realised that I had just assumed all my life that I was going to get married and have children, that I didn't need any qualifications…I remember just feeling so angry…I wasn't happy being a wife and mother of two, having no clue what I was going to do with the rest of my life…I just became a very different person in that process.

Feminism was enacted in the life of the refuge in different ways. Feminist ideals underpinned the ways that workers supported women and children and framed the organizational environment in which they worked. It also informed the relationships they sought to create among themselves and in the wider community. We now turn to the question of how practice informed theory as feminists grappled with domestic violence and tried to make sense of it.

# CHAPTER — 4

# Making sense of domestic violence: History, discourse and lived experience

> I was just thrown into this ocean of domestic
> violence that was incredibly confronting.
> GLENDA BLAKE, 1998[1]

When feminist refuges were first set up in the early 1970s, there were neither the books about domestic violence nor the theorization that exist thirty years later. Refuge workers had to make sense of domestic violence for themselves. It was through work in refuges that feminists not only realized the magnitude of the problem but also began to further develop their analysis in terms of wider social structures and their personal experience of working with domestic violence. Practice informed theory. Hence, in the early years, workers could come to Nardine with very little knowledge, experience or understanding of domestic violence other than some broader commitment to feminism. Today, essential selection criteria for all new workers at refuges include 'demonstrated understanding of domestic violence', indicating that potential staff have to be familiar with particular models that attempt to explain its dynamics and effects.

This chapter considers how understandings of domestic violence have changed over time, beginning with how it was conceptualized before refuges existed. Family law is a window into the lives of women who experienced violent marriages, and this discussion draws partly on the stories of women who sought divorces and judicial separation on the basis of cruelty. What was the relationship between 'cruelty', a ground for divorce, and domestic violence? How did the legal system attempt to deal with violence that under any other circumstances would be considered criminal assault? How was violence between men and women in the privacy of their homes portrayed? What discourses contributed to the existence of domestic violence? And, finally, how had feminism come to understand domestic violence by the 1990s?

## THE LONG HISTORY OF DOMESTIC VIOLENCE

> A woman, a dog and a walnut tree,
> The more you beat them,
> The better they be.[2]

There is a long history of men's rights to 'discipline' their wives. Historically, within many cultural and national traditions, women have been accorded a subordinate position in marital relationships that has been sanctioned by legal, religious and social institutions. Within the British legal tradition from which Australia gained its system of law, women did not have property rights within marriage until the end of the nineteenth century. In other words, married women were unable to own or transact property or to retain income obtained from employment or inheritance. Legally, this property belonged to their husbands. Children were also considered to be in the custody of the father, not the mother.[3] According to this framework, in marriage the 'legal existence of the woman is suspended…or at least is incorporated into that of the man'.[4] As a husband was deemed to be responsible for his wife, he had the right to discipline her. The notorious 'rule of thumb' provided husbands with guidance as to the thickness of a rod that could be used to chastise their wives.[5]

British laws relating to marriage were adopted as the imperial laws of the Swan River Colony. Before 1863, as in Britain, divorce that allowed remarriage was possible only through a special Act of (British) Parliament. From 1863, separation became possible through the *Divorce and Matrimonial Causes Act*, which provided for the hearing and determining of judicial separation and divorce by the Chief Justice in an open Court for Divorce and Matrimonial Causes or in chambers.[6]

Later, and prior to the development of the Family Law Court in the mid-1970s, divorce proceedings were transferred to the Supreme Court of Western Australia. Significantly, 'cruelty', or domestic violence as we might call it now, was from 1863 a ground on which women could seek judicial separation and divorce in Western Australia. However, judicial separation was difficult to achieve, and not just because of economic reasons, which limited most women's access to the legal system. A husband could obtain a divorce simply on the grounds of his wife's adultery; a wife had to prove incestuous adultery, bigamy, rape, sodomy, bestiality, or adultery accompanied by cruelty or desertion for two or more years. Equal grounds were not established until 1911, and even then with considerable debate and disagreement in parliament.[7]

In 1879, the *Divorce and Matrimonial Causes Act* was amended to clarify women's position in relation to judicial separation on the basis of cruelty:

> If a husband shall be convicted summarily or otherwise of an aggravated assault within the meaning of the imperial statute…upon his wife, the Court or Magistrate before whom he shall be so convicted may, if satisfied that the future safety of the wife is in peril, order that the wife shall be no longer bound to cohabit with her husband; and such order shall have the force and effect in all respects of a decree of judicial separation on the grounds of cruelty.[8]

Thus, a woman could be granted judicial separation in the court in which her husband's criminal assault upon her was heard. In addition, he could be ordered to pay maintenance, and the custody of the children given to his wife. Recognition of the existence of violence against wives was beginning, but it was still only in the most extreme cases that women could be assured of some protection from the law in terms of both separating from their violent husbands and gaining long-term financial support for themselves and their children. Australian historian Margaret Grellier, however, argues that this amendment merely recognized established practice and, according to her research, there was no significant increase in applications for judicial separation over the next decade.[9]

A further obstacle to women gaining judicial separation and divorce was that magistrates were required to interpret the extent of cruelty by husbands. As noted by historian Margaret Anderson, underpinning their considerations were beliefs about the desired permanence of marriage and the subordination of women within marriage. During the mid- to late nineteenth century, women were expected to be submissive, dutiful and compliant. Magistrates considered wives' behaviour when ascertaining whether 'cruelty' was justified.[10] Thus, in 1886 His Honour Justice Stone in the Supreme Court of Western Australia could conclude:

> If the wife who is supposed to be in subjection to her husband does not keep herself in that position but tries to keep him under and make him come and cringe to her for anything he may want and if he chooses and attempts to assert his rights as her lawful husband and she then commences to irritate him with her tongue she cannot expect this Court to assist her. Her duty is to try and live peaceably with her husband and to put up to a great extent with his failings and shortcomings. If she has done that and then proves to the Court that notwithstanding all her efforts to make his life peaceable and happy her life or limb is in danger she is entitled to come here and on proof of the facts to get a judicial separation, but until she has established that the Court cannot assist her.[11]

This case, in which Bridget Tant had petitioned her husband of twenty-eight years for judicial separation because of drunkenness and frequent ill treatment, including beating her and chasing her with a hatchet, was dismissed.

Bridget Tant's experience of domestic violence was not an isolated case. Australian historians have documented women's experiences of violent husbands during the nineteenth century.[12] In Western Australia, during this period, reports in police occurrence books and court records provide evidence of the widespread incidence of domestic assaults upon women.[13]

From 1896, there were further legal means through which women could seek redress from 'cruel' husbands. The *Summary Jurisdiction (Married Women) Act 1896* repealed the section quoted of the *Divorce and Matrimonial Causes Act* and introduced a broader definition of 'cruelty'. It continued to include provisions regarding convictions of aggravated assault, and also provided for lesser convictions of assault upon the wife punishable by 'a fine of more than five pounds or…a term of imprisonment exceeding two months'. Furthermore, a wife whose husband had been 'guilty of persistent cruelty' and because of this 'persistent cruelty…caused her to leave and live separately and apart from him' could seek a judicial separation. She was required to apply to two justices of the peace, or to the court if her husband had been convicted. The justices or court could then order a judicial separation, award custody of the children to the wife and demand the payment of maintenance by the husband.[14]

The Summary Jurisdiction (Married Women) Bill passed remarkably uncontroversially through the Western Australian Parliament. 'Cruelty' to wives was conceptualized in terms of marital discord, which was to be the dominant framework of understanding for many decades, rather than in terms of an appreciation of the differences in power exercised by spouses. During the second reading, the Minister for Mines, the Hon. E. H. Wittenoom, noted that

> members will agree that at some period of their lives they have known of differences existing between husband and wife. It often happens, I believe, that husband and wife are unable to live together, and there have been instances, I am informed, of husbands using their wives cruelly and treating them badly.[15]

Some Members of Parliament were aware, however, of the ways in which the legal system could impede women's access to judicial separation and the essential financial support to escape cruelty. Requiring that petitions for judicial separation be taken to the Supreme Court

subjected women to an expense that many could not bear. The Hon.
F. M. Stone reported that he had 'often come across cases where wives
have wanted to obtain separation orders, but have been too poor to
go to the Supreme Court'.[16] Such matters could now be addressed
summarily by two justices in a local Police Court (or Court of Petty
Sessions).

Throughout this period of legislative changes, one clause overrode
the orders of the court:

> No orders shall be made under this Act on the application of a
> married woman if it shall be proved that such married woman has
> committed an act of adultery: Provided that her husband has not
> condoned, or connived at, or by his wilful neglect or misconduct
> conduced to such act of adultery.[17]

In other words, if a wife was adulterous, either before or after the orders
were made, she could be denied maintenance, custody of children and
judicial separation. The expression of wives' sexuality was monitored by
the legal system, and errant behaviour was punished. Men's rights to
control their wives' sexuality were clearly seen as more important than
women's and children's safety and protection.

In reality, many women would never have taken advantage of
these laws because of the cost of litigation, fear of retribution, and
shame at the failure of their marriage. However, my purpose in drawing on them is to highlight a process by which legislation was modified
in response to changing understandings of violence. Increasingly, 'cruelty' was understood as unacceptable within marriage, even if it was still
seen as an aberrant conduct of individual men rather than as a manifestation of masculine power, as it was to be understood by feminists
from the 1970s.

Some women, however, did take advantage of the legislation. In
1905, Adeline Powell successfully sought the dissolution of her marriage and the custody of her child. She stated that during their marriage, her husband had 'treated her with great unkindness and cruelty',
having 'frequently left her without means of support' and 'threatened

her life'. At the time of seeking the divorce, she had left her husband and was working to support herself and the child.[18] In 1920, Elizabeth Cullen successfully sought a divorce from her husband on the grounds of cruelty. He was found guilty of assaulting her and received a six-month sentence in Fremantle Prison.[19] During this period, over the early decades of the twentieth century, domestic violence was understood both as physical 'cruelty'—women being beaten, having things thrown at them and being struck in the face—and in other ways. Women presented affidavits outlining various forms of what could be called emotional abuse, such as threats to their life, and the use of 'gross and filthy language', swearing and abuse. They were also financially and socially controlled, as evidenced in specific court cases, through such mechanisms as being denied money, being left alone on an isolated farm and being left in Perth after the birth of a child.[20]

In 1922, further amendments were instituted through the *Married Women's Protection Act*, repealing the *Summary Jurisdiction (Married Women) Act 1896*. Several changes are evident in relation to 'cruelty'. First, judicial separation, maintenance and custody of children could be sought on the grounds that cruelty had been suffered by the wife or any of her children under 18 years; and, second, the cruelty had to have been inflicted over the preceding six months. The Premier, Sir James Mitchell, in moving the second reading of the Bill in the Legislative Assembly, argued that it

> merely extends the provisions of the law as it now exists, and makes it easier for married women to obtain protection from a husband who is undesirable or neglectful or cruel, or who commits any offence now provided for in the old Act. The Bill makes it easier—and rightly so—for women in such a position to obtain protection.[21]

In particular, according to the Premier, the Bill removed 'the necessity for a conviction for assault or the wife leaving the husband due to his persistent neglect or cruelty';[22] thus, the Bill 'will afford a measure of relief to married women who are badly treated. I hope they are far and few between'.[23] What was not stated in the proposed legislation but had been maintained since the time of Bridget Tant's experience of seeking a divorce was that women's unfeminine behaviour could forfeit their entitlements. As the Premier explained:

> Sometimes, of course, *the man acts under great provocation* as, for instance, *bad cooking or neglect to keep his buttons from falling off.* I ask the House to approve of this measure of protection being made easier for married women while still affording the husband all the reasonable protection he ought to have.[24] [my italics]

To be entitled to legal protection from 'undesirable, neglectful or cruel' husbands, women had to fulfil their side of the bargain. Neglecting to maintain the home and family to the satisfaction of the court was punished severely, given the circumstances of the wives who sought such protection. Furthermore, adultery and drunkenness were behaviours deemed to be unacceptable and could be used against wives to dismiss applications for orders of judicial separation, maintenance and custody of children.

In 1960, the *Married Persons (Summary Relief) Act* repealed the *Married Women's Protection Act*. No longer were protection and financial support available only to wives. There was recognition, for example, that a husband could be dependent on a wife and require 'maintenance' upon separation. (On at least one occasion, a husband had attempted to use the *Married Women's Protection Act* to seek redress from a wife who had 'deserted'. His wife argued that she had left home because of his cruelty, and his application was dismissed.)[25] This Act was further amended as the *Married Persons and Children (Summary Relief) Act 1965*, under which 'relief' could be sought on a number of grounds, including 'cruelty to the complainant or to an infant child of the family'. In parliament, some had high hopes that the legislation would be used to assist couples to reconcile and that legal officers would perform a range of duties including that of marriage counsellor, as suggested by Mr Nulsen:

> This is a very good Bill and ought to improve the relationship between unhappily married couples. The parties to a marriage will

be able to discuss their misunderstandings with the assistance of a magistrate. As a result, there will be a better understanding and a happier relationship.[26]

While it is unclear the extent to which magistrates held the views of those who believed that poor housekeeping was provocation for ill treatment, at least one husband declared his wife to be an unsatisfactory housekeeper. After their marriage in 1951, his wife had sought judicial separation, custody of the children and maintenance on two occasions on the grounds of cruelty and desertion; she then filed a successful application for divorce in 1961. In the divorce proceedings, evidence of sexual, physical, verbal and emotional abuse was presented. According to the wife, the husband

> endeavoured to compel [his wife] to perform abnormal sexual behaviour with him and has sometimes compelled [her] to do so...[He] has continually made excessive demands on [her] for sexual intercourse and when refused has called [her] filthy names and used vile epithets towards her...on many occasions [he] used disgusting expressions to [her] implying that she is a woman of loose morals and habitually committed adultery...[He] has frequently been rude to [her] in front of friends and customers...and has on many occasions belittled her and humiliated her by insulting remarks...After an argument [he] struck [her] and forced her to the floor...[he] grabbed her by the throat and threatened to kill [her] and called her foul names...while [she] was sweeping the floor...he stood on [her] foot and turned with the weight of his body on it.

He denied ever striking her but admitted that there was 'considerable marital discord' because she 'had not been keeping house properly and was refusing to do the housework or cook the meals'.[27]

How did other women use this protective legislation to leave violent marriages and seek maintenance and custody of children? A woman successfully sought a divorce in the Western Australian

Supreme Court in 1962, after she and her children had endured twenty years of violent domestic life. After her husband returned from war service, 'he developed a habit of drinking to excess and repeatedly abusing and threatening [her] and using abusive and threatening language towards her and her children'. This violence increased in intensity and frequency over the years, and included incidents when he struck her and the children and, on at least one occasion, an attack upon her that resulted in her hospitalization. Prior to the birth of their third child, after two daughters, he told her that 'if the child was not a boy, he would bash the child's head against the end of the bed'. During the late 1950s, the woman had sought a judicial separation on two occasions through the *Married Women's Protection Act* on the grounds of cruelty and desertion, but the couple had been reconciled.[28] In another successful application, in 1944, a woman sought a divorce on the basis of her husband's cruelty and habitual drunkenness. She had previously laid several complaints of cruelty during the 1930s using the *Married Women's Protection Act*.[29] Such cases show that the law understood cruelty to include a range of behaviours, including physical and sexual violence, as well as emotional and verbal abuse.

The threat of violence and the engendering of fear were key ways in which husbands maintained power in the home, as evident in this application for divorce lodged at the Supreme Court of Western Australia in 1961. The couple were married in 1956 and lived much of their married life interstate, but the wife returned to Western Australia after leaving the marriage:

> From the outset of the marriage, [he] displayed a hectoring, bullying and possessive nature towards [her]. He would allow her to have no opinions of her own…In the early months of the marriage, [she] endeavoured to claim entitlement to hold views of her own and not be entirely subject to [him] but shortly after she became pregnant with the child of the marriage, [he] assaulted her violently and had to be restrained from continuing his attack…thereafter she remained in constant fear of him and endeavoured to avoid precipitating any outbursts of violence.

> [He] constantly picked on and bullied [her] and when [she] refrained from entering into any argument with [him] she was abused for ignoring the views he was expressing…[He] frequently asserted that a woman was lower than a man and not entitled to her own opinion and that a man's word should be law to his wife and he claimed to be entitled to 'belt [her] if she disagreed with him'…[He] repeatedly made threats to beat [her] if she disagreed with him or failed to obey his instructions.

The threats of harm and of loss of custody of their child were strategies that were used with forceful effect. The husband's conduct was 'constantly abusive and threatening'. She was told 'to pack her things and get out' but was also informed that if she took the child, he would kill her. Furthermore, on his advice, she believed that 'he was the only person with any rights in respect of the custody of the child'. She sought medical assistance for the ill health that resulted from living in such an 'unendurable' environment and was advised that her health would suffer irreparably if she did not leave the marriage. She left, taking the child with her, and successfully sought a divorce and custody of the child.[30]

The *Criminal Code* was used to charge some violent husbands. A woman, married in 1955, had left her husband within the first year of marriage due to his violence. They reconciled, and over the following years she experienced further frequent violence and was intimidated by threats of violence to the extent that she was in a 'state of anxiety, fear and uncertainty'. In 1961, as a result of a severe beating, her husband was convicted of assault, and she successfully sought a divorce. Neighbours submitted witness statements to the divorce proceedings, describing what they saw and heard of the abusive relationship.[31] As this case demonstrates, others were certainly aware of violence in the home. In the proceedings for a divorce granted in 1944 brought on the grounds of cruelty, the wife had turned to neighbours when seeking refuge from her husband's violence.[32]

Over time, legislation was introduced into the Western Australian Parliament that opened up the possibility of abused women leaving their marriages with financial support from their husbands. Considering the level of cruelty experienced by women, it is surprising that the *Criminal Code* was not used more frequently, but this was more to do with the police's unwillingness to intervene in 'private' matters than with the severity of the crimes. Protective legislation such as the *Summary Jurisdiction (Married Women) Act 1896* and subsequent legislation removed, to some extent, the need for women to pursue criminal convictions, as judicial separation could be achieved with evidence of persistent cruelty, which included physical assault as well as sexual and emotional abuse.

However, twentieth-century attempts to reform the law were not received uncritically. For example, during the 1930s, the Maintenance Reform Association for Men, headed by Hector McDonald, campaigned to restrict access to maintenance by wives. In contrast, others thought more should be done for abused wives. Organizations such as the Law Society and the Women Justices Association sought improved conditions for women seeking redress in the courts through the *Married Women's Protection Act.* In 1928, Bessie Rischbieth, a well-known Western Australian feminist, on behalf of the Women Justices Association, suggested that 'matrimonial cases' should not be heard in the Police Courts (or Courts of Petty Sessions). She argued that these public courts kept 'many genuine cases from seeking redress' and recommended a court of 'domestic relationships'. In response to her request, she was advised that Fridays were the 'special day' each week at the Perth Police Court for 'matrimonial cases'. They were heard after all other police matters and in front of a magistrate and a justice of the peace; sometimes the latter was another well-known Western Australian feminist and former Member of Parliament, Edith Cowan, JP. In 1928, 127 such cases had been heard (for reasons including cruelty, adultery and desertion). Not until several decades later, under the amendments instituted in the *Married Persons (Summary Relief) Act 1960*, were separate courts established. The Summary Relief Court dealt specifically with people seeking orders involving judicial separation.[33]

In the late 1950s, there were substantial changes to family law. Federal legislation took over State-based legislation concerned with marriage and divorce, through the amended *Matrimonial Causes Act.*

Further significant changes were to occur in the mid-1970s. From 1975, the *Family Law Act* provided for a single ground for divorce, that of irretrievable breakdown of marriage, otherwise known as 'no-fault' divorce. It was no longer necessary for women to prove that they had experienced 'persistent cruelty' before they could separate legally from their husbands and receive financial support for themselves and their children. Through these changes, the legal process of judicial separation was abolished and relevant legislation repealed. It was intended that the new divorce legislation would

> bring about a more humane and dignified manner of dealing with the problems of marital breakdown without delay and without overburdening the parties with expense.[34]

Many Australian couples took advantage of this easier and simpler route to separation and divorce. In 1976, the number of divorces increased by 140 per cent on 1975 figures and 260 per cent on those of 1974. In 1976, the divorce rate was seven times that of 1960. In the following years, these annual rates declined, and by the mid-1990s the divorce rate was 2.8 per 1,000 population, compared to 4.5 in 1976.[35] In her research of marriage breakdown in the mid-1970s, Australian sociologist Ailsa Burns found that 'husband's cruelty' was one of the main causes of women's marital dissatisfaction.[36]

Despite the evidence presented in criminal, divorce and other courts, and the knowledge of those close to victims of violence, such as the neighbours who took in abused women and their children, even in the 1970s public portrayals of domestic violence were distorted.

## SILENCING DOMESTIC VIOLENCE IN THE 1970s

In the 1970s, silence surrounded women's experiences of domestic violence. The Western Australian Government's Domestic Violence Task Force, which reported in the mid-1980s, examined the context in which domestic violence occurred. The title of the task force's report, *Break the Silence*, was a telling comment on women's experiences. The

Western Australian Government, or at least those representatives whom Nardine dealt with during these early years, were disbelieving about the incidence and magnitude of domestic violence. The 'odd hit' experienced by women was recognized and accepted, but that 'men belted women up night after night' was unimaginable.[37] However, evidence presented to divorce and other courts testified that this did happen.

The Australian Federal Government's Royal Commission on Human Relationships, chaired by Elizabeth Evatt and researched during the mid-1970s, included in its brief an examination of what was called 'family violence'. The commission defined family violence as 'acts of violence by one spouse against the other spouse or against the children' and was concerned primarily with physical violence including rape.[38] The final report of the commission noted that

> [a] certain level of violence has always been accepted as normal in male and female relationships; the wife with the rolling pin, or with a black eye on Saturday night, is familiar comic material. Extreme domestic violence has been regarded as atypical, or characteristic of only certain lower socio-economic groups. Our evidence leads us to believe that family violence is common in Australian society; it occurs across lines of class, race and age. The damage done to women and children is often severe.[39]

The form and level of physical violence reported by women belied the myth that men and women experienced violence equally within relationships. The Royal Commission on Human Relationships, having sought evidence from women's refuges and elsewhere, including crime statistics, was informed that during incidents of domestic violence women had been punched repeatedly, mostly about the head and upper parts of the body, eyes and mouth, slapped, pushed, raped, lacerated, burnt, kicked and strangled, receiving in some cases internal injuries, perforated ear drums, concussion, fractures and gunshot wounds.[40] Domestic violence could be silenced because of a range of factors. The long history of men's rights to discipline their wives meant that this behaviour could be an accepted part of marital relationships. The expectations of women within the family were also a contributing factor. There were strong cultural beliefs about women as wives and mothers, with their primary role being to maintain the family. These cultural expectations were reinforced by the social, legal and economic structures of Australian society, which in turn produced circumstances in which women could be trapped by domestic violence.

Furthermore, images in the popular media clouded and skewed the issue at the time and were to have lasting effects, even three decades later. Domestic violence was portrayed in the media but not from the perspective of women involved in violent and unequal relationships—the women who were soon to crowd into refuges. My survey of cartoon representations of domestic violence from two Western Australian newspapers during the mid-1970s shows that the issue invariably was represented from dominant perspectives. As Australian historian Raymond Evans has stated, cartoons 'defuse the serious nature of gender violence'.[41]

In the cartoons surveyed, domestic violence was commonly depicted in three different ways. In the first version, it was shown as an equal battle between husband and wife. This model lent itself to a cartoon portraying a husband and wife purchasing guns to shoot out their troubles, and which assumed that they both had the same capacity to do so (see p. 100). The Andy Capp cartoons, featured in the *Daily News* throughout the 1970s, are another example in which husband and wife are represented as engaging in violence towards each other, and Mrs Capp gives as good as she gets. These representations of domestic violence came out of a framework of 'marital conflict', which did not recognize what feminists would come to understand as the different positions of power held by husband and wife within their relationship. Instead, 'marital conflict' assumed a 'level playing field' and that both parties were equally responsible for the violence. This model of understanding relationship 'difficulties' was a significant obstacle for the refuge movement and others beginning to develop feminist understandings of women's experiences of domestic violence.

The 'level playing field' model of domestic violence also lent itself to the understanding that men and women both fought but could do it differently—men with their fists, women with their tongues (recall the 'nagging wife')—and that these different approaches were equally effective. Feminists challenged this notion, again drawing on gendered power differences.

A second representation of domestic violence in cartoons portrayed women as the perpetrators of domestic violence. They were pictured as angry, rolling-pin-wielding matrons who physically assaulted their husbands for some minor masculine misdemeanour. Stereotypically, a husband is threatened with a rolling pin as a result of his wife's anger over his late return home (see p. 100). In another cartoon, the husband is depicted as the victim of his wife's violence (see p. 100).

While conceptualizations of domestic violence were largely restricted to physical violence, significantly, emotional abuse of men was also evident in the cartoons. Recall the unmanly 'hen-pecked husband'. In Langoulant's portrayal of family life, the woman has the upper hand (see p. 101). She is portrayed as domineering and unfeminine and he is browbeaten and submissive.

Understandings of femininity and masculinity were a key to these cartoon representations of domestic violence. In the third version, violence against women is portrayed, but it is underscored by an understanding of the proper place of women within marriage. Femininity entailed obedience and subservience, and hence violence that did occur could be understood as being warranted. Presumably, according to these representations of domestic violence, the wife deserved the treatment she received, and because women knew their place within marriage, they were willing and compliant victims. In a Rigby cartoon from 1975 (see p. 101), the wife stands at the door of the bedroom with a broken arm and black eye. We are given no indication of why the husband has beaten her; it is simply taken for granted. Instead, our attention is drawn to his circumstances. The husband is in bed with a buxom, scantily dressed young woman on each side. The issue being addressed was the introduction of the 1975 *Family Law Act*, which required a year's separation prior to divorce.

The use of the concept of 'marital conflict' was a powerful way in which the dynamics of domestic violence were silenced. As discussed, this term, used to describe disharmony between husband and wife,

LEFT: Unknown artist, *Daily News*, 22 January 1975, p. 34. *Courtesy Battye Library*. BELOW LEFT: *Sunday Times*, 31 August 1975, p. 58. *Courtesy the artist; Battye Library*. BELOW RIGHT: *Sunday Times*, 13 October 1974, p. 42. *Courtesy the artist; Battye Library*. OPPOSITE TOP: Allan Langoulant cartoon, *Daily News*, 6 February 1975, p. 36. *Courtesy Allan Langoulant; Battye Library*. OPPOSITE BELOW: Paul Rigby cartoon, *Sunday Times*, 25 May 1975, p. 4. *Courtesy Paul Rigby; Battye Library*

**"Duelling pistols!"**

During the 1970s, cartoons depicted domestic violence in ways that silenced the experiences of women and children. Instead, the portrayal of domestic violence suggested that men and women both engaged in violence towards each other. Alternatively, domestic violence was depicted as undertaken by women: one version was the rolling pin wielding matron and the innocent husband; another was the dominant wife and the 'hen-pecked' husband. Where violence was carried out by men, women were portrayed as willing and deserving victims. Examples of these various representations are shown above and opposite.

"At last women throw off the yoke of apron and tea towel and take their rightful place in the affairs of the world."

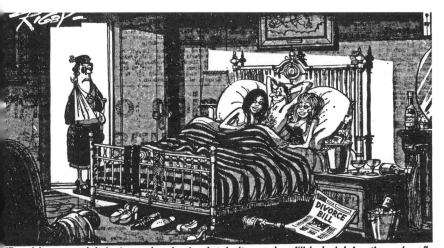

'True, I beat you and don't give you housekeeping, but don't worry dear, I'll be back before the year's up."

assumed that 'conflict' would be experienced equally by men and women, and that it resulted from the inadequate performance of pre-ordained roles within the relationship; these roles were defined, most forcefully, in the work of American sociologist Talcott Parsons. Hence, conflict could readily be resolved by greater success in fulfilling marital obligations. For example, in a study of couples who presented to the Victorian Marriage Guidance Bureau in the early 1970s, conflict was seen to occur as a result of either partner failing to fulfil expected 'sex roles'. This meant that

> if the husband failed to provide for the family adequately and to adopt his leadership and responsibility function; and if the wife was a poor housekeeper, sexually unresponsive, aggressive, dominant or nagging, conflict and disruption were likely to occur.[42]

What is overlooked in this analysis and all the cartoon stereotypes, of course, is that the husband typically had greater power within the relationship. However, my focus here is on how the term 'marital conflict' was used within government departmental reportage to disguise the extent of domestic violence in the community.

While it was not established until some time after the publication of these cartoons, the development of the Western Australian Department for Community Welfare's Crisis Care Unit in 1983 provides a useful government perspective on domestic violence. The Crisis Care Unit, modelled on a South Australian initiative started in 1976, provided 'after hours service…to…people in stressful situations requiring immediate response'. In parliamentary discussions, it was acknowledged that dealing with domestic violence was an important reason for the initiation of the unit. However, the incidence of domestic violence was made invisible within the records collected. In the first week of operation, the 'presenting problem' of one-fifth of calls (21 of 106) was categorized as 'marital discord'.[43] (Clearly, not all would have been situations of domestic violence as feminists came to understand the term, but we can assume that a significant proportion of such calls were, given that in more recent times domestic violence has been identified as a category and consistently makes up about 10 per cent of all calls to the Crisis Care Unit.) This trend continued over the following years, with approximately 15 to 20 per cent of calls being identified as 'marital discord'.

While the Department for Community Welfare did not define 'marital discord' or other category titles used in later years, such as the equally ambiguous 'marital', as early as 1984 it identified domestic violence as a significant but neglected area of work:

> There is no doubt the service provides a service previously unavailable in the community. At the same time, major areas of shortage continue to be apparent. No service such as Crisis Care can provide substitutes for the needs of housing, income maintenance, especially associated with housing problems, and preventive support services for families with teenagers. Furthermore, *many problem areas associated with* cultural minority groups and *women in violence situations*, for example, *have hardly been addressed*. The extension of resources and working liaison with other agencies will be required before the unit's impact reaches these groups.[44] [my italics]

The effect of not naming the violence was to maintain its invisibility and to retain a screen that suggested that discord between husband and wife was an acceptable part of married life that could be readily addressed by adjustment to so-called appropriate 'sex roles'. Terms such as 'marital conflict' were used to refer to situations that included 'abuse or battering', where the ultimate goal of social work intervention was to effect reconciliation.[45] While refuge workers' priority was the safety of women and children, others in the welfare field at this time were more concerned with the preservation of the family unit, regardless of the cost to its individual members.

Despite the silence of government documents, during the 1970s and 1980s departmental workers must have seen women and children experiencing domestic violence. For example, the Family Court Counselling Service had been set up in 1976, under the provisions of the federal *Family Law Act*, with the aim of assisting disputing parties 'to resolve their differences'.[46] These 'differences' were not uncommonly manifested violently, as former Family Court counsellor Eversley Ruth explained:

> At the point of marital breakdown, physical expression of anger is very common. In fact, counsellors working with divorce would probably expect such violence to be more common than not. Whether it persists during the marriage and becomes public at breakdown is not known. It is at least as likely that at the point of breakdown, physical violence erupts as part of the hot anger cycle of the grief process. It is therefore not surprising that therapists working with unhappy marriages meet a great number of reported violent attacks.[47]

Refuge workers in the 1970s would have found it difficult to reconcile the stories of women coming into their care with either the term 'marital conflict' or the cartoon images prevailing in the popular media.

## DEVELOPING UNDERSTANDINGS OF DOMESTIC VIOLENCE

What 'mental and/or physical violence and cruelty', as was first elaborated when setting up Nardine, meant for women quickly became apparent to workers at the refuge. In 1974, when the refuge opened, a year before the introduction of the 'no-fault' *Family Law Act*, women continued to appear before the Supreme Court seeking divorce on the grounds of cruelty. These women's stories provide further insights into experiences of violence in the home at this time.

As in cases that had come before the courts in earlier decades, women described their experiences of physical, sexual, verbal and emotional abuse within marriage. These forms of violence included threats, the use of obscene terms as verbal abuse, and being repeatedly struck about the body, punched around the face, held by the throat, and beaten to the ground, causing bruising to ribs, arms and face—forms of violence that were recorded in divorce proceedings, inflicted by a medical practitioner against his wife.[48] In another case, a tradesman was in gaol at the time of his wife's successful application for divorce. During their life together, after marrying in 1944, he had repeatedly assaulted her, causing injuries requiring hospitalization; he had even pushed her in front of a train. He had also damaged their home and furniture and attempted to burn down the house. This woman had in 1970 sought protection through the Summary Relief Court.[49]

There is some evidence of changing attitudes to violence in marriage and acceptable standards of feminine behaviour. As noted, the legislation at this time specified that women engaged in sexual relationships outside their marriage at the risk of jeopardizing court orders. In at least one case in 1974, a woman did admit to an adulterous relationship and successfully sought a divorce. Even though the husband had not condoned the adultery, the marriage was dissolved on the grounds of cruelty. She had been assaulted by him, he had made 'filthy and disgusting remarks' to her and he had been 'abusive and argumentative' in their home and with others. At other times, he had kicked her with his work boots, and grabbed her, forced her to the floor and then forced her up by her hair. He had accused her of 'having something on with another man', said he 'would fix her' and went for his rifle. On numerous occasions, he had threatened to shoot her. She experienced 'grave mental and physical distress' and left with their two children.[50]

Maggie Lawson, a former resident at Nardine, recalled her experience of domestic violence. While living in an abusive relationship, her life was focused on her family and preventing others from knowing about the violence occurring in her home. She described herself as 'a mass of nerves, trembling from head to foot' when she came to the refuge in 1976. She did not understand that she was not to blame for the violence. Lawson said that she and others at the refuge at this time were

scared and put down and had absolutely no confidence in ourselves and just believing everything that was told to us: that we were stupid, ignorant, deserved to be beaten, mad, all those things were thrown at us. Yes, you start to believe it when they're thrown at you a lot of times.[51]

Just as consciousness raising had informed feminist analysis, so did the practice of working with women and hearing their stories. For many workers, hearing women's stories about the violence in their marriages was a revelation. While elsewhere in the wider community, domestic violence continued to be understood largely as an aberration until well into the 1980s, refuge workers were appalled at the extent and severity of violence perpetrated against women. Daphne Smith recalled how she was confronted by domestic violence upon beginning work at Nardine:

I was very shocked when I started working there to see how women were being treated. I never knew that this was going on…in the first few weeks that I was at the refuge I saw people who were physically abused. And one woman I remembered in particular had a plug of hair pulled out of her head that was about the size of a tennis ball…And I thought, 'my God, why would a man who says he loves a woman treat her like that?'[52]

Glenda Blake acknowledged that refuge work was 'new territory' for her and others:

We were certainly feeling our way in terms of what domestic violence was about. What the implications were for women and children, what we were trying to achieve as a refuge movement, what we felt about perpetrators of domestic violence…I don't honestly think that I even intellectualised what domestic violence meant for me at that time. I think I had a really gut feeling and gut reaction to what domestic violence was, based on the experiences of women and children coming through the doors of Nardine.

Working with survivors of domestic violence gave workers a deeper understanding of the circumstances of women's experiences.

Diana Warnock, for example, became more aware of the structural reasons behind women's reluctance to leave violent relationships.[53] Inadequate child-care, lack of employment opportunities and limited financial resources were clearly impediments to women's independence.

Some refuge workers, like Deborah Dearnley and Daphne Smith, had read some feminist literature before they came to Nardine in the late 1970s and early 1980s. They tried to make sense of domestic violence in line with the available theorization, as Dearnley explained:

> When I came to work at Nardine I was reading a lot of feminist literature and just beginning to identify as a feminist…I came to the refuge with no idea of what a refuge was or how I would work in this environment. I was very young and very naive. What I experienced through working at Nardine began to fit with the feminist theory I was reading. I began to understand on a practical level what the oppression of women in our society could lead to…that to a large extent the society we lived in condoned the use of violence against women.[54]

Anna Spencer, a resident at Nardine, had not come to the refuge as a result of domestic violence but rather had sought refuge due to homelessness after the break-up of her marriage. Like other workers, she developed understandings of domestic violence based on her later experiences of working at the refuge and placing it in a wider context of feminine disadvantage:

> Back in the 60s [sic] people knew about Germaine Greer and that sort of stuff…it was all quite remote and I was aware things were happening but they weren't touching me…We'd all prefer to think that things like domestic violence don't happen but if you realise that they are, they're there, they're real, you have to cope with it, and deal with it, and to help, hopefully, play some kind of practical part. So it was quite a quick education for me to wake up to it. I began to feel quite comfortable about it because I had grown up like so many women of my generation thinking that so many things were unfair, as far as the difference between gender was

concerned. I had a brother and the expectations of what I was supposed to do were so vastly different and I couldn't understand that. It didn't make any sense to me, and women for years felt like that and so this was really saying that all those feelings that you've had are quite justifiable. It's the way the average woman felt and you had the right to feel like that and a right to do something about it.[55]

In attempting to inform the wider community about their observations of the extent and severity of domestic violence, Nardine's workers were met with disbelief and defensiveness. Daphne Smith recalled her experiences of public speaking in the early 1980s:

We gave talks on domestic violence. Oh, when I think about what it was like in those days, we used to be quite provocative [in] the things that we used to say. But some of our audiences were so aggressive toward us, it was a nightmare. I can remember one time Wendy [Revell] and I went to the School of Nursing…We thought they were going to come down and punch us because we told them that men are violent toward women and they didn't want to believe it.

Others thought that domestic violence was a difficult matter that should be confined to the privacy of marital relationships, as observed by Kay Hallahan, a former Member of Parliament and, earlier in her career, a policewoman. She recalled being out on patrol with male police officers during the 1970s. When a notice of a 'domestic' came over the radio, 'it was very clear that the priority that the call was given was to drop it to the bottom of the list that those officers had to deal with on that particular shift'.[56]

Existing theories about domestic violence ignored differences in power between men and women, absolved men of responsibility for their actions, and blamed women for the violence. Commonly, it was believed that violence only occurred in working-class families or that men were only violent when they were drunk. It was also widely accepted that men learnt domestic violence behaviours from their fathers and grew up to be violent husbands, and that girls who saw their mothers beaten would grow up to be victims of violence in their own marital relationships. Others argued that women caused the violence or indeed wanted to be beaten.[57]

Refuge workers challenged these theories. Domestic violence, they believed, could be understood differently within an empowerment rather than a protective model and when the personal was made political. Women could be protected from physical, sexual and emotional violence, but they might not be able to maintain their safety. Protection was limited in its capacity to change anything for individual women or the wider society in the longer term. Empowerment, however, was concerned with both personal and social change. It provided for a wider understanding of domestic violence that gave space to the crippling effects of emotional abuse, which could result in a 'reign of terror' where there was no need for physical violence.[58] Whether physically carried out, or threatened, these forms of violence limited women's capacity to take control of their own lives. Empowerment, then, was about working with the effects of the violence, as well as its context. Reminding others of the scope, severity and extent of violence, including physical, financial, emotional and sexual forms, was an ongoing task of the refuge movement.

In the late 1970s, the 'cycle of violence' model became widely adopted as a way of understanding the dynamics of domestic violence. Instead of relying on 'marital discord' to explain specific incidents of violence in relationships, it moved towards a model where men learnt to manage their anger. It did not, however, account for controlling behaviours used by violent partners as an ongoing part of a relationship.[59] From the late 1980s, the 'power and control' model developed by the Domestic Abuse Intervention Project in Duluth, Minnesota, has informed understandings of domestic violence. Its framework is captured in this definition of domestic violence:

[T]he patterned and repeated use of coercive and controlling behaviour to limit, direct and shape a partner's thoughts, feelings and actions. An array of power and control tactics is used along a continuum in concert with one another.[60]

The need for greater criminalization also informed developing understandings of domestic violence, despite the limitations of the *Criminal Code*. The *Criminal Code* provided only for physical assault (and only later sexual assault) within marriage, and feminists had much broader understandings of domestic violence. Historically, police were reluctant to intervene in 'private' matters, and feminists had gone the route of refuges, removing women and children from the site of violence rather than insisting (with likely considerable failure) that the man be removed and restrained from retaliation. In recent years, there have been increasing attempts to criminalize domestic violence. For example, the introduction of stalking legislation within the *Criminal Code* has specific implications for domestic violence. A Family Violence Court was established in the northern suburbs of Perth in 1999 with the aim of improving the criminal justice response to domestic violence.[61] Amendments to restraining orders legislation have also attempted to increase women's safety.[62] Coordination within the criminal justice system and integration across other sectors are an important goal in ensuring improved responses to those affected by domestic violence.[63]

## BREAKING UP FAMILIES

A man's home is his castle.[64]

Again and again, understandings of domestic violence clashed with ideas about the family. Refuges were considered to break up families— particularly at a time when domestic violence was seen as 'marital discord' rather than as a crime. Forceful discourses of the family worked against feminist understandings of domestic violence based on structural analyses of gendered power and of women's capacity for empowerment and self-determination.

Even before refuges began taking in women leaving their family homes, there was a long history of feminism being identified with 'breaking up families', among other social ills. From the 1940s

in the context of the Cold War, feminism was increasingly identified with subversive forces, threatening the stability of family and community. It was blamed for the rising tide of divorce and family breakdown, the proliferation of unmarried motherhood, women going out to work, and men's loss of power.[65]

Ideologies concerned with motherhood, femininity and the family are significant to the consideration of women's position within the home and family at this time. In postwar Australia, the nuclear family—consisting of 'a heterosexual couple and their immediate offspring, where the husband was the breadwinner and the wife the housekeeper and child-rearer'—was considered to be 'the building brick of Australian society'. Politically, socially and economically, the family was conceptualized as the nuclear family, as delineated by American sociologist Talcott Parsons.[66] Within this model, husbands/fathers and wives/mothers performed roles intended to ensure 'the socialisation of children and the stabilisation of adult personality', with these being desired goals of family life. Parsons theorized that women are the 'expressive' carers and men the 'instrumental' leaders. A woman as 'a helpmate…releases tension within the family and acts as support for the father as provider'. In contrast, a man, as the leader, 'guides the family through the rocks and shoals of the world outside the family'.[67]

These functionalist views, that the nuclear family was 'functional' to each of its members and wider society, informed social welfare policy and underpinned the desire to keep families together, at virtually any cost. They were held by people in positions of power within government. In 1980, the Minister for Community Welfare, Bill Hassell, stated that

[t]he family as the basic unit of our society, has never been under greater threat. A variety of social factors including the high

divorce rate, a declining birth-rate, the changing role of women and the growing number of single parent families, are undermining the family as the cornerstone of the society.[68]

Others, however, were sceptical. Robert Hetherington, a Labor Member of the Legislative Council from the late 1970s, argued that as revealed by the work of women's refuges, 'the "domestic bliss" of the nuclear family has often resulted in battered wives and children'.[69]

By the end of the 1980s, there was increasing awareness of the potentially deleterious effects of family life. This is evident in the goals of two key government departments working with Western Australian families. The newly established Office of the Family, with ministerial responsibility to the Premier and Minister for the Family, Carmen Lawrence, maintained the view that the family was 'a basic social institution' but that, at the same time, 'the rights and interests of family members as individuals' should not be overlooked.[70] More explicitly, the domestic violence policy of the Department for Community Services stated that 'it may be inappropriate to maintain a family unit where domestic violence…is occurring'.[71]

As we have seen, a significant expectation of women within the nuclear family was their role of ensuring harmony. Clearly, the presence of 'marital conflict' was an indication of women's failure to perform their roles as wives.

How did the image of refuges 'breaking up families' develop, and what were the underpinning ideologies that sustained such an idea? Feminist writers of the 1970s attacked the Parsonian model of the family and argued that it was the 'chief site of the oppression of women'.[72] Drawing on Marxist notions, they demonstrated that the nuclear family was 'a power hierarchy, with the father having economic power as he either owns the means of production or earns a wage over which he has control'. In addition, he had authority, status and prestige due to his gendered position within social structures.[73] At the same time, the gender division of labour within the family produced circumstances in which women performed unpaid labour in the home and men were able to have their interests met at the expense of those of their wives whose at-home nurturing and caring prohibits equality of involvement in the public spheres of paid work, politics and other institutions of society.[74]

Closely aligned with the ideology of the family, which had the potential to trap women in circumstances of domestic violence, were conceptualizations of femininity and motherhood that further entrenched particular views of women and their place in the family. According to Australian sociologist Betsy Wearing, based on research she conducted with mothers of pre-school-aged children in the 1970s:

> [T]he ideologies of motherhood and femininity are closely enmeshed so that a woman's sense of femininity is entwined with the potential (or actuality) of motherhood. To be considered a mature, balanced, fulfilled adult, a woman should be a mother.[75]

Furthermore:

> A 'good' mother is always available to her children, she spends time with them, guides, supports, encourages and corrects as well as loving and caring for them physically. She is also responsible for the cleanliness of their home environment. A 'good' mother is unselfish, she puts her children's needs before her own.[76]

Hence, due to understandings of the family, women could believe that staying in a violent relationship 'for the sake of the children' was preferable to leaving and seeking safety elsewhere with them. She could put 'her children's needs before her own' and remain in a violent relationship.

In contrast, radical feminist understandings of domestic violence and feminine disadvantage challenged traditional ideas about the family, as indicated by this comment from a Women's Liberation newsletter of 1974:

From babyhood we are brainwashed with the myth of dependent motherhood, the purpose of which isolates and alienates us from all that society values—money, success, power. By bringing women together we discover the faults not only in us, as individuals, but in being female in a male-centred culture.[77]

At Nardine, such radical feminist ideas informed the ways workers tried to make sense of domestic violence:

So there was a real taking on of the whole patriarchal system…in terms of the roles that we assigned to men and women in the family unit and the sorts of things that women were meant to do and put up with. And how those systems allowed women to be violated in their own homes and almost condoned that violation.[78]

For lesbians coming out of the women's liberation movement, the critique of traditional notions of femininity and the family could be understood in terms of the effects of dichotomous 'sex roles' and 'compulsory heterosexuality'.[79] Hence, given feminist refuges' misgivings about the institution of the family and its deleterious effects on women, it is not surprising that those who worked in refuges were likely to hold the most radical views about sexuality and to challenge 'compulsory heterosexuality'. Radical feminist lesbians were attracted to work at Nardine. And lesbians were an easy target for those wishing to discredit the work of refuges at a time when lesbianism was highly stigmatized in the wider community. One refuge, at least, was referred to as a 'lesbian brothel', and at times Nardine had graffiti proclaiming the perceived sexuality of the refuge workers on its very visible front fence.[80] The prospect of women leaving their marriages to live with other women in a refuge, and then possibly having lesbian relationships, was a challenge to understandings of the family and women's sexuality.

Conceptualizations of domestic violence have changed over time, within legal and popular cultural frameworks as well as through feminist theorization. At least legally, with the term 'cruelty', there was recognition given to women's experiences of physical, emotional and sexual assault within the home for a century before 1970s feminists took on the term 'domestic violence'. What these legal understandings could not do, however, was represent the extent of the violence, because few women had recourse to legal remedies. Popular images of violence in the home distorted representations of the experiences of women and children, and ideologies of the family and women's place within it were forceful deterrents to alternative understandings. From the 1970s, then, one of the goals of refuge workers was to inform the community about the severity and extent of domestic violence. These attempts would lead to a new range of responses to domestic violence in the 1980s and 1990s.

# CHAPTER 5

# Breaking the silence: Responses to domestic violence in the 1980s

> The Department's [domestic violence] policy then is based on the knowledge that domestic violence is a manifestation of the prejudice and inequality that exists between many men and women in our society.
> DEPARTMENT FOR COMMUNITY SERVICES, *DOMESTIC VIOLENCE POLICY*, C. 1990

By 1990, the Western Australian Government was naming domestic violence and incorporating feminist understandings into its policies. What changes occurred over the 1980s to make this possible? This chapter investigates the politicization of domestic violence during this decade by looking at refuge workers' struggle for funding for their services and the impact that this had; developments concerning welfare support; and attempts to eliminate domestic violence. In particular, two key milestones of the 1980s were to have a significant long-term impact on the work of refuges and the wider domestic violence field. In relation to funding, the introduction of the Supported Accommodation Assistance Program (SAAP), while resisted at first because of its focus on homelessness rather than on violence against women, provided secure, long-term funding for refuges. In relation to welfare and other responses to domestic violence, the Western Australian Government's Domestic Violence Task Force and its report, *Break the Silence*, officially identified the magnitude of the problem and began the task of improving and coordinating responses to domestic violence.

The concept of 'breaking the silence' was not just about changes in official responses to domestic violence; it was also about changing wider community perceptions. In the late 1980s, the Commonwealth Office of the Status of Women conducted the first Australian survey on community attitudes towards domestic violence, which resulted in a nation-wide community education campaign being run. Other sources of contemporary community attitudes were local responses to the prospect of a women's refuge moving into a neighbourhood—some strongly resistant, others more understanding.

## POLITICAL LOBBYING AND GOVERNMENT ACTION

In the latter part of the 1980s, domestic violence began to be taken up by the Western Australian Government as a social issue requiring action. Most notably, this was in response to the 1985 Domestic Violence Task Force. Prior to this, however, refuges were 'a very lonely voice' when it came to speaking out about domestic violence.[1] It was, for example, more than ten years after Nardine was established in 1974 before there was a coordinated and formalized response to domestic violence in Western Australia. This can be at least partly attributed to the existence of long-term conservative governments at both State and federal levels for much of this decade. In opposition, the Labor Party had incorporated policies into its platform that were sympathetic to the demands of the women's movement, and so when there were changes of government federally and at the State level in 1983, there were opportunities for significant change. Federally, these changes concerned the funding of refuges and, later, national community education campaigns.

In 1983, in Western Australia, the conservative Liberal–National coalition was replaced by Labor, led by the progressive Brian Burke. The scene was set for substantial social change, and refuges had high hopes. Much work had been done prior to the change of government. During these years, when little seemed to be changing at departmental level, Women's Refuge Group founders Michelle Scott and Lois Gatley, among others, were 'extraordinary campaigners and advocates for the women's refuge movement'.[2] Like the women who worked to establish Nardine, these women were skilled lobbyists. The Women's Refuge Group had been established in 1977, and Michelle Scott recalled how it played a very significant policy role. We had all these committees. We produced papers on everything. We'd be going to the State Housing Commission. We had some pretty infamous meetings with Community Welfare with Directors and Director Generals and those sorts of people…We used to go to Canberra a lot, meet with Ministers [and shadow ministers] and all the bureaucrats…We would demand to see [them]…There was a lot of that sort of pressure going on even though there wasn't a big shift in funding till Labor came in. That was the end of a big and competent campaign.[3]

By the time of the change of government, there was a 'very well developed, identified need' in relation to domestic violence because of 'all the work those people had put in'.[4]

Throughout the early years, it was apparent that work with families was the priority of refuges, and Nardine had very quickly become caught up in dealing with individual crises. However, there were some who were also involved in political action. At Nardine, in response to the scale of violence, some workers, including Daphne Smith, made a commitment to work towards wider social change through the Women's Refuge Group. Smith explained:

[T]hat was part of the reason why I started going outside the refuge. I thought, we can't fix this up one by one…we were always talking about the Band-Aid approach…But every one woman that you put the Band-Aid on, that helps her to start off into a new direction. Even the women who go back, they're healed to some extent by the knowledge that they can leave and that there is a support system out there, that they can get out. But I wanted to do more than work with women in the refuge.[5]

The pressure that the Women's Refuge Group exerted produced a range of changes, including an investigation into domestic violence. More immediately, lobbyists questioned government policy at a time when policy was not necessarily identifiable and, if it was, could be discretionary and unwritten. Michelle Scott explained:

> In Community Welfare there was an emergency relief program. There were no guidelines for who could be eligible and under what circumstances…The same with the State Housing Commission and their emergency housing programme…if they liked you, you might go to the top of the list. If they didn't, you didn't know where you might go…

Scott's comments are reinforced by a finding of the 1987 evaluation of SAAP-funded women's refuges. The evaluator, Ludo McFerran, recommended that 'Homeswest produces clear written guidelines for criteria for priority listing, which includes domestic violence'.[6]

Another major area of concern was police response to domestic violence. The police played a significant role in domestic violence, but there was a reluctance by many officers to criminalize men's assaults upon their female partners. The lack of importance attributed to domestic violence was evident in the ways in which some police officers failed to support those who were the victims of what, in any other circumstances, would have been considered serious crimes. For example, refuge workers observed police taking no action on violence by not charging perpetrators and not supporting women. Glenda Blake recounted the injustices she witnessed. She recalled

> going with the police to women's houses and having the police just stand back and not offer any assistance at all. In fact, some times [the police would] take the perpetrator aside and have a chat to him as though he was one of their best mates.

And during this display of Australian mateship, the refuge worker would be assisting the woman to move some basic items out of the house—in effect, 'moving their whole lives' into 'sub-standard, cold and isolated' housing.[7] Further accounts were reported to the Domestic

Violence Task Force, and recommendations were made concerning the training of police and their interventions in domestic violence situations.[8]

During the 1970s and 1980s, the lack of understanding of domestic violence within government departments and in the wider community, tensions around funding, the resistance to data collection and the inadequacy of provision of services by other agencies fuelled antagonistic relationships between feminist refuges and the State. As Cath Munro recalled, Nardine's workers were thought to be a 'load of rat bags' by those in the wider community and government, as well as by some in the refuge movement.[9] From this radical position, Nardine's workers used their power to bring about social change concerning domestic violence.

In the 1980s, there was an 'us and them' mentality at Nardine. Deborah Dearnley, who worked there from the late 1970s to the early 1980s, identified the need to protect women as a central concern of the refuge. In relation to domestic violence, Dearnley believed that 'the wider society was not interested and was not well-informed'.[10] Thus, at this time, a 'closed door approach' was taken at Nardine, and this characterized its relationship with government agencies such as the Department for Community Welfare (in the 1980s, to become the Department for Community Services), the State Housing Commission (later to become Homeswest), the police, and the two primary sources of funding, the Health Department and, later, SAAP within Community Welfare. (In recent years, with improved understandings of domestic violence and its effects, more open and constructive working relationships have been developed.)

This 'closed door approach' was evident in a range of ways. For example, data collection for the funding body was vigorously resisted by Nardine.[11] As Sue Allen recalled, 'we didn't want to be answerable to any of their male dominated patriarchal requirements'.[12] These 'male dominated patriarchal requirements' included informing the Health Department of statistics regarding the numbers of women and children, their Aboriginality or otherwise, and their dates of arrival and departure.[13] In retrospect, from the perspective that government should be accountable for the expenditure of funds, these do not seem unreasonable requests, but, to Nardine's feminists at the time, they were unwelcome and unnecessary intrusions into the work of the refuge. There was also considerable distrust because of the ways in which such evidence could be used to construct minimum, and what were perceived as inadequate, funding levels. Worse still was the fear that Nardine might lose its funding. There were ongoing battles about data collection, and the refuge's policy was that minimal information would be provided. On reflection, however, Dearnley thought that Nardine might have done itself a disservice because of its expertise in identifying needs and developing innovative service delivery strategies.

Access to housing was a priority concern for refuge workers, and they took action in a range of ways to change government policies and practices. During the 1980s, workers from Nardine and other representatives from the Women's Refuge Group met with the State Minister for Housing to discuss waiting lists for emergency accommodation provided by the State Housing Commission. Racism compounded the difficulties experienced by Indigenous women seeking accommodation, and Nardine saw stark evidence of this discrimination.[14] For Indigenous women, it resulted in acute housing problems and long stays in refuges while awaiting alternative accommodation, sometimes up to six months. These and other concerns about the long-term housing needs of women and children in refuges were highlighted in the Women's Refuge Group submission to the Domestic Violence Task Force and also in McFerran's 1987 evaluation of Western Australian women's refuges. In particular, McFerran recommended that Homeswest accept applications from women living in their marital home who wished to leave due to circumstances of domestic violence. She reported that in some Homeswest offices, applications would not be taken from women before they left home, for fear of staff being accused of 'breaking up families'. This even happened in towns where there was no refuge or other inexpensive, safe accommodation to which women could move and from which they could lodge applications.[15] Instead of 'breaking up families', these practices reinforced women's sense of powerlessness and supported situations in which women and children could continue to experience violence in their own homes.

Nardine also took more militant action concerning the provision of emergency accommodation. Deborah Dearnley recalled an incident in about 1982 involving one of Nardine's clients who had been on the State Housing Commission waiting list for many months. Nardine found an empty State house, and the woman and her children moved in. Workers took turns staying with them, waiting for the State Housing Commission to act. Eventually, the police were called and the woman was evicted as a squatter. Several Nardine workers were arrested, charged with trespass and received twelve-month good behaviour bonds. Housing for women leaving the refuge continued to be a major problem throughout the 1980s and beyond.

Despite these tensions, there were allies within government who, at times, were able to support Nardine's position. This was particularly

Nardine workers Kedy Kristal, Wendy Revell and Genna Claire, with children and others, protesting about long waits for 'priority' housing for women leaving refuges, c. 1983. *Courtesy* West Australian

apparent from the middle years of the decade, with a State Labor government and increasing numbers of 'femocrats' attempting to introduce change through government policies. During the 1980s, the establishment of the Women's Information and Referral Exchange, the Women's Advisory Council and the Women's Interests Division, and the presence of advisers on women's services in key government departments, were all indicators of increasing feminist activity within bureaucracy, and the government's increasing willingness to bring about social change in relation to domestic violence. For example, in 1984 the Women's Advisory Council published a booklet entitled *Women in Crisis*, which had been prepared by the Women's Refuge Group and Women Lawyers of WA. *Women in Crisis* provided valuable information to women leaving home because of domestic violence. It was reprinted several times and translated into ten languages. In the same year, the Women's Advisory Council published another booklet entitled *Women and Family Law*, which included information on injunctions and restraining orders and listed, among other relevant services, women's refuges in Western Australia. These initiatives were noteworthy contributions and evidence of coalitions of feminists working together to assist women and children experiencing domestic violence. At the same time, the Women's Information and Referral Exchange, opened in 1984, assisted many women with information about domestic violence services and provided guidance on obtaining restraining orders against violent partners.

During the mid-1980s, some of Nardine's workers, including Kedy Kristal, Deborah Dearnley and Wendy Revell, were centrally involved in setting up another refuge in Perth specifically for young women. They had identified a need for the service and were also aware that government funding might become available. While still working at Nardine, this group and others established the new service, to be known as the Young Single Women's Refuge, unfunded and unpaid. Like Nardine, 'Young Singles' was set up as a collective and took a radical feminist approach.[16]

Although major changes did not occur until the mid- to late 1980s, there were discernible shifts in understandings of domestic

violence by some sections of the community, other than refuge workers and their feminist allies, before this time. Nor did domestic violence
go unnoticed by Members of Parliament, some of whom were clearly
allies of the refuge movement. From the mid-1970s, there had been
some discussion of refuge funding and the capacity of existing refuges
to accommodate the numbers of women and children seeking assistance. Continuing this supportive trend, Robert Hetherington, Labor
Member of the Legislative Council, argued in 1980 that 'the whole
problem of domestic violence and violence in our society is important
and urgent. We can solve this problem only by spending more money
and setting up new agencies'.[17] In a ground-breaking speech to the
Upper House in 1981, Labor Legislative Council Member Lyla Elliott
put forward a motion that, if passed and acted upon, could have
brought about far-reaching changes in response to domestic violence
much earlier. With a minority of Labor members in the Legislative
Council, it was not passed. Instead, it was amended by government
members, which gave them, according to Labor member Peter Dowding, 'a little pat on the back'.[18] Elliott was 'extremely disappointed' with
the government's response to her motion and 'thought this was one
issue on which this Chamber could reach a degree of unanimity'.[19]
Elliott's intention had been to request the government to

1.  enact legislation to enable the appropriate laws to be
    changed to give greater protection to victims of domestic
    violence;
2.  urge the Federal Government to amend the Family Law Act
    so as to attach a power of arrest by Police for breach of an
    injunction either against threatened violence or against
    approaching the applicant or the place where the applicant
    resides;
3.  establish in the current financial year a Crisis Care Unit
    whose function would include the provision of intervention
    and counselling services related to domestic violence;
4.  increase the funding of women's refuges in this State to
    ensure:

(a)    the ability to accommodate all cases requiring emergency accommodation;
(b)    adequate staffing of refuges;
(c)    appropriate wages for refuge workers;
(d)    recognition of individual needs of each refuge.[20]

In formulating these requests, Elliott drew upon, among other literature, the recommendations of the New South Wales Government's 1981 task force on domestic violence and called for Western Australia's own domestic violence task force. This was not to eventuate for another four years. She also drew on the work of the South Australian Crisis Care Unit, established in 1976, and acknowledged that the Western Australian Government had been investigating the possibility of setting up such a service since 1979, at least partly because of the capacity of such a unit to assist in situations of domestic violence. However, Western Australia did not get a Crisis Care Unit until 1983, with the delay attributed to 'budgetary constraints'.[21]

The setting up of the Crisis Care Unit was a significant milestone in the development of services to women and children escaping domestic violence in providing assistance out of office hours. Although there were not the resources to deal with it adequately, domestic violence was identified early on as a high priority area for the new service. In 1982, parliament was informed that the unit would

> assist in the management of domestic disputes and violence and would work in close conjunction with the police. The service would respond to family crisis situations which require quick action to relieve a situation of extreme stress to children or parents.[22]

Indeed, Kay Hallahan, MLC, reported in July 1983 that 'while this unit is available to meet any emergency, its field workers are specifically qualified to intervene in situations of domestic violence'.[23] But even though domestic violence was named as such by others at the time, it remained invisible behind the category 'marital discord' in the Crisis

Care Unit's records for the first five years (as discussed in chapter 4). The Department for Community Welfare's 1984 Annual Report advised, for example, that in the Crisis Care Unit's first year of operation, 22 per cent of calls were related to 'problems associated with marriage' but that the needs of 'women in violent situations…have hardly been addressed'.[24] So while some parliamentarians were discussing domestic violence, informed by the lobbying of the women's refuge movement, the department seemingly remained unable to identify it.

Even if government departments did not appear to understand the magnitude of the problem during the early 1980s, others were aware of community concern. For example, by 1982 domestic violence had been identified as an important enough concern among politicians and those aspiring to political life for people of opposing political parties to vie for positions on the management committee of a newly establishing women's refuge, Starick House. Kay Hallahan recalled how the Labor candidate for the Legislative Assembly seat of Gosnells, Yvonne Henderson, competed with a Liberal Party candidate, Bill Mitchell, widely regarded as the 'right hand man' to the Premier, Charles Court. After a 'tactical and hard fought' campaign, Henderson and Hallahan were successful in becoming management committee members. Mitchell attempted to maintain his profile in the area by setting up a foundation to raise money for the refuge.

Lyla Elliott's unsuccessful proposal that legislation be enacted to provide greater protection to victims of domestic violence provoked lengthy debate and revealed a range of attitudes to domestic violence. Liberal parliamentarians were against such action, for several reasons. Margaret McAleer, MLC, who led the government's response to Elliott's motion, argued that 'Governments never will be able to legislate marital bliss'.[25] To this, Labor member Robert Hetherington responded, 'It is all very well to say we cannot stop domestic violence by legislation, nor can we stop murder by legislation; but that does not mean we do not pass legislation against murder'.[26] McAleer argued that protective legislation did exist, in the form of the *Criminal Code*. It provided opportunities for prosecution against violence in the home, McAleer asserted, but because of the necessity for 'a reliable independent witness' and because in the majority of cases such a person was not present, there seemed to be 'little point in prosecuting'. In addition, McAleer observed, 'in many cases a woman is reluctant to complain or press charges'. Thus, and in summary, 'as far as criminal legislation is concerned, there is provision for domestic violence as it related to the protection of women and children; but the requirements of justice limit its application'.[27] Indeed, its application has been highly limited: rarely, it seems, is the *Criminal Code* used to prosecute domestic violence.

Civil law was an alternative response, and McAleer informed the Legislative Council that married women could seek protection through injunctions (or restraining orders) from the Family Court. The Federal Government was, at the time, following a review of the *Family Law Act*, considering amendments to increase police powers in relation to injunctions. Others in Opposition argued that these amendments would take too long, were inadequate and applied only to married women and not to those in de facto relationships, and that further legislation was therefore required.[28]

Dissatisfaction with the existing legislation was recognized, despite the lack of support for Elliott's motion in the Legislative Council. In 1982, the Attorney General, I. G. Medcalf, announced the establishment of an advisory committee to consider legislation to protect victims of domestic violence. This committee, however, did not include community representation. Elliott unsuccessfully led a deputation of women's groups to the Attorney General, in an effort to broaden the committee membership and to widen the terms of reference to include services and prevention strategies related to domestic violence.[29] In 1983, changes to the *Justices Act* were introduced that attempted to provide increased accessibility to, and usefulness of, restraining orders for women seeking assistance because of domestic violence.[30]

There was further acknowledgment from those in government that change was needed. The Attorney General advised that responses to domestic violence involve a new attitude on the part of the police in that they will be required to make complaints and do things that they have never done before in relation to domestic violence, in intervening in some situations.

As far as the Department for Community Welfare is concerned, it is involved in a far deeper way than ever before. Instead of being a little distant and simply tendering advice, officers of the department have to go in and assist the parties to sort out their troubles in this area.[31]

In other States of Australia, government task forces or other forms of research into and review of domestic violence were undertaken in the early 1980s: New South Wales and South Australia in 1981 and the Northern Territory in 1983. Western Australia's investigation did not begin until 1985.[32] However, even if some thought it a rather belated response, it laid the groundwork for responses to domestic violence over the next decade and put the issue firmly on the State's political agenda.

## DOMESTIC VIOLENCE TASK FORCE

In February 1985, the Western Australian Government's Domestic Violence Task Force was announced by the Premier, Brian Burke. Its report, *Break the Silence*, was published in January 1986. According to chairperson Lyla Elliott, the task force was 'government recognition that domestic violence is a matter of public concern and not an issue to be hidden behind closed doors'.[33] The inquiry's aims were:

(i)    To estimate the extent to which domestic violence is a problem in the community generally, and in particular for: migrant families, Aboriginal communities, women and children living in isolated situations

(ii)   To evaluate the effectiveness of existing laws and services dealing with domestic violence, with particular reference to:

(a)   the operation of State and Commonwealth laws in the protection of women and children in situations of domestic violence

(b)   the adequacy of services provided by: the police, the government welfare services, non-government organizations

(c)   the scope for rationalising existing laws and services and improving their effectiveness and coordination

(iii)  To evaluate procedures developed or proposed in other jurisdictions, with a view to considering their application in Western Australia.[34]

Members of the task force were representatives from the government and non-government sectors and included Liza Newby from the Women's Interests Division of the Department of Premier and Cabinet, Christine Wheeler from the Attorney General's Department, Dot Goodrick from the Department for Community Services, Lois Gatley from the Women's Refuge Group, Tracey Summerfield from the Community Legal Centres, Dot Bagshaw from the Black Women's Movement, Annalisa Emamy from the Multicultural and Ethnic Affairs Commission and Peter Ayling from the Police Department. As Lois Gatley recalled, the task force 'brought together some people who didn't usually sit at the same table: women's refuges and police officers didn't usually sit together and talk before that'.[35]

The report of the task force drew on a wide range of literature and other sources including other Australian Government investigations into domestic violence. A recently released report of the so-called Anderson Committee, which had reviewed amendments to the Family Court in relation to domestic violence but was limited to police powers and did not involve community participation, was also consulted. In addition to textual sources, importantly, the task force invited the participation of the wider community by seeking public submissions, making country visits, undertaking studies of the police and other relevant agencies, and conducting two public surveys—one promoted through the *Sunday Times* and the other a phone-in. In addition, two papers examining domestic violence in relation to migrant women and Indigenous women were prepared for the task force, and educational institutions that taught nursing, medicine, social work, psychology and law contributed their relevant curricula (none of these courses were found to teach about domestic violence). Thirty-one public submissions were received (plus others from unidentified 'victims'). Those contributing included individuals and agencies from within the Department for Community Services, WEL, the Women's Refuge Group, the Marriage Guidance Council, Women's Health Care House, the Women Lawyers Association, the Alcohol and Drug Authority, Holyoake, the Australian Psychological Society and the Australian Association of Social Workers. Nearly 400 callers participated in the phone-in, more than 400 questionnaires from the *Sunday Times* survey were completed and others spoke to task force members at public meetings about their experiences. These public consultations provided invaluable information about the experiences of those living and working with domestic violence. In particular, for many victim/survivors, speaking at the phone-in was the first time they had ever told anyone about their life with domestic violence. As Lyla Elliott explained, at this time

> the great majority of victims were trapped in a situation where they put up with the violence and didn't talk about it. The Task Force, I believe, changed all that with its message 'break the silence'. It gave victims the chance to talk to someone and let them know that they didn't have to suffer in silence. Many of the nearly 1000 victims that approached the Task Force hadn't contacted anyone for help. They thought it was their problem. Very few had obtained restraining orders. In very few cases was the perpetrator charged with assault. Some victims had suffered in silence for twenty years. So it was the first time many victims were made aware that they were not alone and they could get help.[36]

Lois Gatley, the Women's Refuge Group representative on the task force, travelled to the north of the State to consult with local people about domestic violence. In the mid-1980s, there were no refuges throughout the vast Kimberley region, nor any other identified domestic violence services, and police and welfare officers were reluctant or unable to respond. Even though Gatley had by this time worked in refuges for some years and was aware of the magnitude and severity of domestic violence, particularly against Indigenous women, she recalled that the 'level of violence, the depth of it, the volume of it, was just so extreme'. She met with women and heard stories of 'terrible violence' for which there was 'no response':

> The Welfare couldn't manage it. The Welfare was engulfed with issues of child abuse and protection, let alone poverty, let alone what was happening to the mothers of those children. The Department of Aboriginal Affairs of the day had no way of responding to it. The police viewed violence against women as part of their culture, they didn't see anything wrong in it. What you might do is lock up the drunk people, chuck them in the cells overnight but you certainly didn't take any stance about it.

A priority concern that came out of the task force was Indigenous women experiencing domestic violence in rural and remote communities. One tangible outcome was the development of a refuge in Broome, already initiated at the time of Gatley's visit and established by the end of the 1980s, and since then a further five women's refuges have been developed in the Kimberley region.

Like Gatley, Elliott was shocked by the level of violence against women:

> When I was appointed to the Task Force I don't think I was prepared for the enormity of the suffering that women had experienced over such a long time. I had been hearing stories second hand from refuge workers but it wasn't until I was involved in the Task Force and started hearing directly from the victims themselves that I realised how awful the problem was and the severity of the violence. That was my most outstanding impression and a disbelief that something like this could have been going on for so

long and the public not being aware that it was happening until the women's movement really brought it to the surface.

Evidence of the value of refuges to women and children escaping domestic violence was presented in *Break the Silence*. According to the agency survey conducted by the task force, women's refuges were identified as the most used referral points in the first instance, and also the most commonly contacted in the second and third.[37] In the words of those who had used them, women's refuges had been 'the only place to turn to'.[38]

The task force delivered 103 recommendations across a broad range of areas including police, family law, women's refuges, health, housing, education and welfare. There was some acknowledgment that not everyone would agree with these recommendations. In the foreword to the report, task force chairperson Lyla Elliott commented:

> If any of the recommendations may be considered controversial, it should be remembered that any social reform that challenges long held prejudices, attitudes or vested interests will initially always tend to be so. No doubt, the nineteenth century legislation removing the husband's legal authority to beat his wife was in this category.[39]

An important need identified by the task force was for coordinated responses to domestic violence that were much broader than 'welfare', as Michelle Scott argued:

> So you didn't just say domestic violence is the Minister for Community Services' responsibility. But you said, it's the government's responsibility and the community's responsibility and various government agencies have a responsibility…so it's built on the early work and that whole policy push that this is something that government should be responding to in a holistic way.

In November 1987, an interdepartmental committee known as the Domestic Violence Coordinating Committee was set up to oversee

Nardine workers, including Cath Munro, Julie Potter, Lyn Nelson, Joan Groves, Annie Farrell and Libby Best, and residents, breaking the silence of domestic violence, c. 1989. *Courtesy Nardine collection*

the implementation of the 103 recommendations of the task force. Chaired by the director of the Women's Interests Division in the Department of Premier and Cabinet, it included representatives for the Ministers for Health, Police and Emergency Services, Housing and Community Services, the Attorney General's Department, the migrant and Indigenous communities, the Women's Refuge Group and the Women Lawyers Association. Representatives for the Ministers for Education and Multicultural Affairs and the Royal College of General Practitioners were included later. The committee's brief was, in collaboration with the relevant ministers and their departments, to review health and housing matters related to domestic violence, develop education programs for schools and the wider community, prepare a handbook on restraining orders, provide assistance to self-help groups, develop staff training, establish services to rural families, and review procedures for obtaining and implementing restraining orders.[40] By May 1988, Pam Beggs, representing the Minister for Community Services, reported that

> [c]hanges have been introduced to police in-service course and recruit training to include information on restraining orders. Police routine orders have been revised to clarify police powers and responsibilities in domestic violence situations and to emphasise the criminal nature of domestic violence. Changes to the law regarding restraining orders are being drafted, a health policy statement is being developed and in-service training courses for Homeswest staff are under way. Research is being undertaken into the establishment of an Intervention Unit in the Police Department and a community education program on domestic violence. Staffing and resources have been increased in the Crisis Care Unit and funding and staffing increases have been made to women's refuges. Counselling programs for violent men will be developed and appropriate services and support for women in violent domestic situations are under consideration.[41]

## MAKING CHANGES AT DEPARTMENTAL LEVEL

The task force recommendations had particular impact on those departments most directly involved in providing services related to domestic violence. The Department for Community Services, previously known as Community Welfare and formed from a partial amalgamation of Child Welfare and Native Welfare in 1972, had undergone increasing professionalization through the employment of university-trained social workers and psychologists during the late 1970s and 1980s.[42] The department was at the front line in providing welfare support to women experiencing domestic violence, through the work of the Crisis Care Unit and divisional offices, and had statutory obligations in relation to the care, protection and safety of children. Furthermore, from the mid-1980s, the department administered the funding of women's refuges.

Agencies and individuals within Community Services who contributed submissions to the task force included those from the Women and Welfare Committee, staff and the coordinator of the Crisis Care Unit, the senior clinical psychologist, the Midland divisional office, the Parent Help Centre, and the clinical psychologist at Nyandi, a female juvenile detention centre. This was the largest number of submissions from any one agency.[43] Clearly, there was concern about domestic violence from across the department.

During the period immediately after the task force, from 1986 to 1989, Kay Hallahan was Minister for Community Services. She was a supportive, sympathetic minister with an understanding of the issues, born out of her previous work as a police officer and her involvement in the setting up of Starick House women's refuge. Her parliamentary colleague Judyth Watson, who chaired the Domestic Violence Coordinating Committee and reported to Hallahan as Minister for the Family for much of the committee's existence, believed that Hallahan's 'personal dedication' to the issue of domestic violence, and the wider government support through Premiers Brian Burke and Peter Dowding, were of great significance in ensuring that changes at departmental level did happen.[44]

What, then, were some of the concerns raised by the task force and what were the departmental responses? As well as specific recommendations related to the Crisis Care Unit and the funding of refuges, there were several recommendations concerning the department's activities more broadly. First, it was recommended that domestic violence be acknowledged as a priority issue for the department, and that policies and practice guidelines be developed and staff training undertaken to sensitize all departmental workers to the issue. Furthermore, it was recommended that the Department for Community Services develop closer links with relevant government and non-government agencies, to better meet the needs of women and children living with domestic violence.

The task force's concern that Community Services acknowledge domestic violence was well founded. During the 1970s and early 1980s, no mention of 'domestic violence', or other terms to suggest its existence, was made in its predecessor's Annual Reports. Even though the refuges tell stories of their overflow of women and children at this time, domestic violence was seemingly something that either the department did not deal with or remained unnamed and invisible within this source of official documentation. However, departmental workers must have seen women and children experiencing domestic violence. Violence, for example, was commonly noted by the department's Family Court Counselling Service. Women applied to the department for financial assistance to leave violent marriages through Administrative Instruction 222, and, during the early 1970s, women had sought temporary financial support upon separation from their violent partners before being eligible for the Single Mothers' Benefit. In each of these ways, departmental officers would have been exposed to women's experiences of domestic violence. Where some acknowledgment might have been made of its existence, the gendered nature of domestic violence was not recognized until well into the 1980s, when feminist understandings of power inequalities between men and women were incorporated into government policy.

During the late 1980s, the development of departmental policy began to make domestic violence visible, and practice guidelines were formulated in 1990.[45] Prior to this, though, the 1987 departmental strategic planning document, *Directions*, had provided indications of increasing sensitivity to domestic violence and the articulation of departmental responsibilities in the area. While the department's role was specified within section 10 of the *Community Services Act* as 'promoting individual and family welfare in the community' and 'preventing the disruption of the welfare of individuals and families in the community and mitigating the effects of any disruption', its philosophy was more nuanced. It said that Community Services would undertake 'its Charter in a manner that is…conducive to maintaining the family unit, *as appropriate*' (my italics), which had come about as a result of 'greater community awareness and debate on sensitive and serious welfare problems such as child abuse and domestic violence'.[46] Thus, the goal of the department was to improve support and develop resources for individuals who are victims of domestic violence; enhance and develop services for families in which domestic violence and child maltreatment is occurring; develop prevention and community awareness programmes to assist families at risk of and in which domestic violence and child maltreatment is occurring or might occur.[47]

An administrative instruction with important implications for women and children in situations of domestic violence makes a useful case study of change in the Department for Community Services. Administrative Instruction 222, 'Assistance to women leaving home', provided for financial assistance to women for travel costs associated with leaving a situation of domestic violence in a country area. The Domestic Violence Task Force found that the instruction lacked clarity and granted considerable discretion to departmental staff, resulting in 'inconsistency in service-provision and inconvenience to those seeking assistance'.[48] While the task force raised concerns about the focus on fathers' access to their children, a Family Court matter, it noted that the instruction was under review. In parliament in November 1986, the minister representing the Minister for Community Services, Keith Wilson, reported that Administrative Instruction 222 had been reviewed as a result of a request from the task force and that 'the new procedures give staff clearer guidelines in providing more support and protection to women and children of domestic violence'.[49] However, in McFerran's 1987 evaluation of women's refuges, this instruction was again noted as a matter for concern. Even though the department's responsibility was to provide assistance to transport victims of domestic violence to safety, there continued to be inappropriate responses in the field. McFerran reported:

> The common attitude was that DCS officers could not assist women to leave their homes, as they could be accused of *breaking up the family*. One officer even believed this was against the law...One remote country refuge described women with children hitchhiking to the refuge from outlying areas. They had never known a DCS officer help a woman to the refuge.[50] [my italics]

In 1990, the department's newly launched *Spouse Abuse: Guidelines to Practice* made explicit the circumstances in which women and children could be given financial assistance 'to obtain safety and protection if they have been harmed or fear harm in a violent relationship'. Financial assistance was available for transport to a refuge or any other safe place, to get urgent medical treatment, to seek police assistance or to obtain a restraining order. Furthermore, assistance was available to cover the cost of emergency accommodation where no refuge was available and for meals and other expenses under those circumstances.[51]

Crisis Care Unit staffing was increased as a result of recommendations of the task force. Two workers were on duty at all times, enabling a worker to accompany police officers to women's homes, and all workers in the unit were to receive specialized training in domestic violence. The Crisis Care Unit also provided advice on available refuge beds and could pay for alternative accommodation if refuges were full and for transport to accommodation.[52]

## FUNDING OF WOMEN'S REFUGES

Through the 1980s, the funding of women's refuges was a site of tension between workers and those in government. From the late 1970s, the Commonwealth Government had provided 75 per cent of funds to refuges, and in all States except Western Australia and Queensland the State had provided the balance. Initially, atypically, Nardine was supported with 100 per cent funding by the government, because it was an independent organization without a sponsoring agency. However, in 1979 this changed and Nardine became subject to the same funding guidelines as all other Western Australian refuges: the State Government contributed 12.5 per cent and the remaining 12.5 per cent was to be provided by the refuges.[53] The government's rationale was that refuges had to demonstrate that they had public support, from whom they would gain the balance of funding. As Ray Young, MLA, Minister for Health, explained:

> If an organisation has true community support, then this should
> be demonstrated by an ability to attract donations to be used as a
> contribution towards the cost of operating the refuge.[54]

However, women and children who used Nardine's services did not
usually have the financial resources to pay, and Nardine's submissions
showed that most residents struggled to contribute even minimally to
the costs of their stay in the refuge.

For independent agencies like Nardine with little access to funds
other than those from the government, cuts in funding came straight
out of workers' wages.[55] As Lyla Elliott, MLC, noted, the requirement
to raise funds placed 'a heavy burden on the workers...many of whom
are forced to donate all or the major part of their wages to keep the
refuges open'.[56] Alternatively, as Mike Barnett, a Labor Member of
the Legislative Assembly, observed, this strategy placed 'hardship...on
the voluntary [sic] workers at these institutions who as a result have to
spend much of their time fundraising instead of manning [sic] the
refuges'.[57]

The low funding of refuges was underpinned by several assumptions held by those who provided the funding. On the one hand, refuge
work was devalued and its necessity was challenged. On the other, there
was an assumption that even if it was valuable work, it need not be
paid. Refuge workers resisted both these interpretations. They insisted
that refuge work was important and necessary work, and that the inadequate funding of women's work was unacceptable. These two themes
figure consistently throughout the battles for increased levels of refuge
funding.

Members of Parliament were lobbied and a media campaign was
run, informing the community that workers were donating their own
wages to run the refuge. The refuges did get community support, and
in 1981 the campaign successfully resulted in the required 12.5 per
cent contribution by refuges being dropped. This was a dubious
victory, because the total funding did not increase: all that had happened was that the State Government no longer insisted on refuges

contributing 12.5 per cent. Not surprisingly, funding overall remained inadequate. At the same time, the Commonwealth had handed over responsibility to the State, and refuge funding came out of the reduced State health budget.[58] Again, politicians expressed their concerns. Robert Hetherington, MLC, commented that refuges were

> in grave financial difficulties; some want to expand, but are struggling to keep together what they already have. Some are run by idealist young women who are feeling defeated. They may give up. Certainly the turnover of voluntary staff at refuges is very high. They need cosseting and helping.[59]

Lobbying continued, and in the following two State budgets existing refuges received substantial increases in funding and new country refuges were supported. However, even after these increases, Western Australian refuges, having experienced years of extreme financial difficulty, were left with a 'bitter legacy'.[60]

At times during the 1980s, Nardine received the highest level of government funding of the Western Australian refuges, partly as a result of its history within government funding programs and partly because of the size of its premises and the number of families accommodated.[61] However, government funding was inadequate to pay decent wages to the number of workers needed to cover Nardine's large twenty-four hour service and to address the costs required to maintain the deteriorating buildings. Further public funds were sought, such as through the annual street appeal, raising on average $800 each year—insufficient to cover even a month's operating costs at the time.[62] Nardine's financial circumstances were also more precarious than those of many of the other refuges in Western Australia, which were supported through local councils, religious organizations or other larger sponsoring agencies. Cath Munro, a worker at Nardine through the 1980s, recalled that during this period the refuge was never sure whether it would get its next quarterly funding cheque and that it believed there was always the risk it would be closed down. Even when Nardine was most vulnerable, however, it maintained its radical feminist edge.

Sue Allen's vivid memories of the refuge in the late 1970s and early 1980s reflect the appalling conditions under which women lived and worked due to the limitations on funding:

> We were terribly overcrowded both with people and cock-roaches…We used to try everything to get rid of the cockroaches. We had different people come in, exterminators and god knows what. But there were people everywhere. I mean the rooms used to hold a lot more people than they were ever designed for. So it was sort of mayhem around dinner time. There'd be 30 people and screaming kids…but I used to hate it when the last woman went to bed because when it was quiet all the cockroaches came out…

Glenda Blake, who worked at Nardine during the early 1980s, also recalled the physical state of the refuge:

> At the time that the refuge operated from Vincent Street it was probably the most run down building that I have ever seen in my life…it was dirty and there were holes in the walls and the floor coverings were coming up.

Allen's and Blake's memories of Nardine confirm some of the worst images of women's refuges.[63] This picture of the refuge as overcrowded, dirty and run-down was a deterrent to some women taking up its services. In a submission seeking funds to construct a purpose-built refuge in 1985, it is clear that the physical state of the building had affected some residents. A Nardine worker noted that

> [r]egrettably, a not inconsiderable number of women have come into Nardine requiring shelter, and subsequently left because they found the physical dilapidation of the house too difficult to cope with.

However, Daphne Smith, a Nardine worker during the early 1980s, offered an alternative view of the refuge at this time. She recalled the building as being solid and secure and adequately providing the basic necessities. Despite the concerns expressed by some workers and residents, the refuge was a place of safety for many women.

In 1983, new Labor governments—both State and Commonwealth—were elected, among other issues, on promises of increased funding to refuges. But Nardine was disappointed. In the 1984 Annual Report to the Commissioner for Public Health, Nardine's feminists described the impact of the change of government:

> In our Annual Report we would like to make some positive comments about our improved position as a result of a change of Government and thus of governmental attitude. A change from anti-women's refuges to a pledge of 'proper and adequate funding levels for refuges'. However, we have discovered almost no difference in attitude or in funding, except that it has worsened.

They noted the lack of funding for capital improvements including those for the buildings, furniture, fences and fittings.

Increased funding to refuges became available in 1984 through the newly formed Women's Emergency Services Program (WESP), an outcome of a Labor election promise. Jointly funded by State and Commonwealth governments, it incorporated funding to refuges as well as other related women's services, and administration was transferred to the Department for Community Welfare. In 1985, SAAP commenced, underpinned by the Commonwealth *Supported Accommodation Assistance Act*. Much to the disgust of the women's refuge movement, WESP was incorporated into SAAP. This change was strongly resisted by refuges, as SAAP's central focus was homelessness, not domestic violence. The refuge movement was committed to a women's services funding program, but in the end bureaucrats won the day.[64] In retrospect, some now argue that the long-term security of SAAP, held firm by its legislative base, has served women's refuges well.[65]

From 1984, with the establishment of WESP and after its incorporation into SAAP, women's refuges were involved in program and policy development. Representatives from each of the Western

Australian refuges, with staff from State and Commonwealth welfare and housing departments, met monthly. One of their major functions was to recommend 'funding levels and priorities for WESP' to the SAAP/ Crisis Accommodation Program Coordinating Committee, which in turn was answerable to the State and Commonwealth ministers. This high level of involvement of agencies in decision-making was unique in Australia.[66] WESP ran in this consultative manner until the end of the first five-year SAAP agreement (known as SAAP mark I) in 1989. SAAP mark II then came into force for a further five years, but it brought substantial and unpopular changes to the advisory structure. WESP as such was dismantled. From then on, women's refuges were no longer identified as a block within the funding program; instead, all services, including youth, family and men's services and women's refuges, were dealt with administratively on a regional basis. Women's refuges were no longer locked into the funding policy and program development processes.

Funding of women's refuges was identified by the Domestic Violence Task Force in 1986. Increased funding was recommended, in order to increase staffing overall, extend follow-up to women after they left and provide better allocation of child support across refuges. The task force recommended ongoing funding for specialist services for women of non-English backgrounds and the employment of more Indigenous women in refuges, and identified the need for additional country refuges, for funding of relief staff to enable refuge workers to attend training, and for refuge workers' involvement in the development of departmental policy and practice guidelines.

An evaluation of the Western Australian refuges party to the first SAAP funding agreement was conducted in 1987 by long-time refuge worker Ludo McFerran, who had undertaken two similar reviews in New South Wales. The evaluation and its report, entitled *Beyond the Image*, were greeted with enthusiasm by refuge workers, who saw them as a way to review their work, an opportunity to develop new strategies for the future, and a mechanism through which to inform the government of the work done by refuges and the need for further social action around domestic violence. Some of the key issues that came out of the evaluation concerned children and Indigenous women. Other recommendations, such as the need for increased public housing stock and improved police and welfare responses, reiterated those of the Domestic Violence Task Force of the year before. McFerran's evaluation formed part of the national review of SAAP undertaken by Colleen Chesterman in the late 1980s. According to the review:

> WESP and women's refuges are clearly associated by the community and by bureaucrats with family violence. They are perceived as the government and community's major response to family violence. While they have been very successful in raising public awareness of the issue, they have not had the authority or the resources to tackle all aspects of family violence.[67]

The review found that the refuge model had been successful in assisting women and children escaping domestic violence, but that greater diversity of services was required. It recommended increasing the number of refuges, where needed, and the further development of services including independent units with outreach support, and supported halfway housing funded through SAAP.[68]

In the 1990 budget, nearly $5 million was allocated to funding women's refuges in Western Australia. Even though there were now nine refuges in country areas—in Albany, Bunbury, Broome, Geraldton, Port Hedland, Kalgoorlie, Karratha, Narrogin and Northam—and a further eighteen in Perth, the vast distances between towns and communities meant that there were still women in many parts of Western Australia who had severely limited access to domestic violence support services.[69]

The tensions over funding levels brought domestic violence to the attention of government, particularly given the vocal and unrelenting approach of the refuge movement. It was not only the impact on refuge workers' pay and conditions that was of concern; the lack of recognition of domestic violence as a significant issue requiring social change affected the provision of services to women as they attempted to move on from the refuge.

## 'A SAY, A CHOICE, A FAIR GO'

At the Commonwealth level, domestic violence did not go unnoticed. As well as funding refuges, the Commonwealth Government made other forays into the field. As early as 1979, the Australian Institute of Criminology held a first national conference on 'violence in the family', which was repeated on a larger scale in 1985 at the request of the Attorney General.

Coming out of the 1985 international conference in Nairobi held to review the United Nations Decade for Women, 1975–85, *The Nairobi Forward Looking Strategies for the Advancement of Women* was an action plan for further progress to the year 2000. Internationally, domestic violence was placed on the political agenda at this conference by the widening of the goal entitled 'peace' to include 'peace at home'.[70] Pat Giles, Western Australian Labor Senator and long-time member of the Western Australian women's movement, led the Australian delegation to the Nairobi conference. The Australian Government's response to the Nairobi document was to develop an action plan entitled *A Say, a Choice, a Fair Go: The Government's National Agenda for Women*. Its purpose was to 'open up opportunities to all women by giving women a choice, a say and a fair go', by developing 'an integrated plan for Government action to improve further the status of women'.[71] During 1986, wide-ranging consultations were undertaken throughout Australia on topics including women's access to education and training, participation in the paid work force, child-care, health and income security. In the first instance, violence was not identified as a specific topic within the consultations on women's health, but it emerged as a 'priority concern'. Thus, the government's action plan, developed in response to community consultation, included specific objectives and strategies relating to reducing the incidence of domestic violence, changing community attitudes, further developing support services for victims and improving police responses.[72] The National Agenda for Women, in concluding, stated that '[b]y the year 2000…the Government hopes to see an Australia which is free from violence in the home…'.[73] Like the aim of the refuge workers who hoped to 'do themselves out of a job', this goal has proved difficult to achieve.

In 1987, the Commonwealth–State Coordinating Task Force on Domestic Violence was formed with representatives from Commonwealth and State governments. Its principal role was to provide advice to the Commonwealth Office of the Status of Women on its national domestic violence campaign, to be run over three years.[74] In a major survey of community attitudes to domestic violence, 'a disquieting level of community tolerance of violence by men against their wives' was revealed. In summary, the community attitudes survey found:

–   One in three Australians regard domestic violence as a private matter.
–   One in five condone the use of physical violence by a man against his wife.
–   One in two do not view verbal abuse as domestic violence.
–   One in four do not consider it violent if a man threatens his wife, and one in ten do not view pushing and shoving as violence.
–   Very few people view psychological and emotional abuse as violence.
–   Many people believe that women 'ask for it' or 'must have done something to deserve it'.
–   Two out of three think a woman can easily leave a violent relationship.[75]

Consequently, in 1989 a campaign to change community attitudes was run, leading up to the National Domestic Violence Awareness Month in April that year, launched by the Prime Minister, Bob Hawke. This campaign, the first of its kind, acknowledged the existence of domestic violence. It included television advertisements, billboards and posters, and had a budget of nearly $1 million.[76] Poster images of a woman with a black eye were placed on bus shelters and other prominent public sites—evidence of government willingness to break the silence and take a stand against domestic violence. Further education programs in the following year targeted Indigenous and rural communities and people of non-English-speaking backgrounds, and a booklet was produced by the Western Australian branch of the Royal College of General Practitioners to assist doctors to work with domestic violence.[77] Despite these attempts to improve community understanding of the issue, in a national survey of women of non-English-speaking backgrounds conducted in 1990, 70 per cent 'had little idea about how Australian law might assist victims of domestic violence'.[78]

In 1990, a new committee, the National Committee on Violence Against Women, took over the work of the Commonwealth–State Coordinating Task Force. A second survey, broadened to consider violence against women rather than exclusively domestic violence, was conducted in 1995 (see chapter 6).

## GRAPPLING WITH COMMUNITY ATTITUDES

Given the 1987 national community attitudes survey's revelation that a substantial proportion of the population denied that domestic violence was a problem, it is not surprising that there was heated opposition to refuges moving into residential neighbourhoods. Not only did refuges have a poor image as dirty and crowded; they also had a bad name for 'breaking up families'. For many, it seems, refuges were at best unnecessary and at worst a challenge to deeply held views about family life and relationships between men and women.

In 1984, Nardine came up against these and other attitudes when it embarked on finding a new home. The houses in Vincent Street that had been the site of the refuge for a decade were badly in need of considerable repair work, and the owner was threatening to sell. Nardine investigated the possibility of purchasing the buildings, but the deal fell through. Without secure funding, but with several applications pending, Nardine then attempted to purchase a building in Kimberley Street in Leederville, but, due to protests by local residents, the City of Perth rejected its application for special approval to run a refuge in a residential area. In 1985, Nardine successfully sought funding through the newly created Crisis Accommodation Program to buy land and build a new refuge. Later that year, $120,000 was paid for three adjoining blocks in a south-eastern suburb of Perth. However, planning took several more years, and building did not commence until 1990. Before the refuge could find a place to settle, it had to move twice to other rented properties. In 1991, after years of planning, negotiating and hard work, the new Nardine was opened. But this had not happened without considerable debate in the local communities with whom the refuge had temporarily resided and in the neighbourhood where it came to stay.

In 1985, in response to the announcement that Nardine was seeking approval from the Perth City Council to establish a refuge in their neighbourhood, some local residents presented a petition outlining their objections. They stated that the proposal was

totally abhorrent…for the following very forceful reasons.

1.  […] is generally recognised as a Senior Citizen's area, with all amenities in the neighbourhood catering mainly for retired couples, widows or widowers.

2.  Most of the houses in the immediate vicinity are occupied by elderly people, in some cases by widows living alone…It is therefore quite unreasonable to plant in their midst a Refuge for young women with children from broken homes…

3.  The replacement of three well-adjusted families by ten to twelve under extreme stress will automatically convert a quiet neighbourhood of elderly or middle-aged citizens into an area of noise and fear…[79]

The local paper, the *Southern Gazette*, reported that locals, including those who had signed the petition, were concerned that 'if drunken husbands came looking for wives and children, their [the locals'] safety would be at risk'.[80] However, other residents were sympathetic to the planned refuge. The *Southern Gazette* ran an opinion poll on the proposal, and among those who responded was Mrs Barbara Holmes, an 80-year-old resident, who hoped that the refuge would be approved because she considered refuges 'necessary in any area'. She believed that 'brutes of men who bashed their wives should be punished' and that women and children should have 'somewhere safe to go'. Another elderly local resident, Mrs Sybil Matthews, agreed. She reported that when she was younger, there were no such services and that it was 'a step forward that families can now go to refuges until their home situation is sorted out'.[81]

Meanwhile, Nardine's workers were busily attempting to inform the neighbourhood about the work of the refuge and the likely minimal effects on those living nearby, including the couple who initiated the petition. Refuge workers reassured local residents that refuges were not noisy, nor did they engender fear in those living in their vicinity. They also lobbied Perth City councillors. While the petition required consideration by the council's Town Planning Committee, Nardine's development application was approved subject to high fencing and landscape screening to 'enhance the preservation of local residential amenity'.[82]

Planning for the refuge building took considerable time and included initial sketches by architecture students from Curtin University, followed by the work of architect Richard Hammond. In April 1988, with architectural plans finalized, Nardine had to resubmit an application for development, as the 1985 approval had expired. Again, the refuge ran into local residents' protests. Some objected to the refuge development on the grounds that it would 'have the potential to bring violent domestic disputes into the area' and 'devalue surrounding residential properties'. As in 1985, there was also some concern that it was inappropriate to locate a refuge in an area that had a number of elderly citizens. Council made contact with landowners to further ascertain local opinions: of 145 approached, seventy-seven objected and twenty-seven accepted the proposal. Letters of support were received from the local police, Members of Parliament, and government and non-government agencies with whom Nardine worked, and the refuge again attempted to work with local residents to inform them of the refuge's work and the likely minimal impact. Even though the proposal could not be rejected on planning grounds, according to the City Planner, the Town Planning Committee recommended that it be refused because of 'the many objections'. While some councillors supported the refuge, including Councillor Jack Marks, who spoke in favour, seeking 'a more caring attitude', the majority opposed the development and the application was refused.[83] In August 1988, Nardine was informed that the development was unsuitable due to 'the use being contrary to the orderly and proper planning of the locality by virtue of increased traffic and disturbance'.[84] Nardine appealed the decision to the Minister for Planning, Pam Beggs. After examining a Town Planning Appeal Committee report on the matter, Beggs upheld the appeal, arguing that, on the one hand, she had

> noted the number of objections that have been lodged against the proposed refuge and the strong feelings that have been aroused by the proposal, but, on the other…it has to be recognised that there is a very real need for the provision of suitable premises to house homeless women as referred to in the appeal submission.[85]

During this time, Nardine had had temporary accommodation in Albany Highway, East Victoria Park. Workers moved there in late 1987, believing it would be for less than a year before they moved to their new refuge; however, because of the delays, the lease at this address expired and another temporary home had to be found. Homeswest provided a house in Berwick Street, but a City of Perth special approval to operate there as a refuge was required. Nardine workers again canvassed local residents, providing them with information about the refuge. Some local people, who were concerned about preserving their 'residential quality of life', circulated a letter advising residents to record their objection with the City of Perth. The anonymous letter informed 'fellow residents' that

> refuges more often than not result in the male partners of the women affected attending at the refuge demanding to see the women concerned or the children and making loud and abusive threats often while drunk. Frequently violence is threatened to persons or property and often carried out. This results in the police being called to attend and so forth.[86]

Refuge worker Julie Potter speaking at the opening of Nardine's new home, 1991.
*Courtesy Nardine collection*

The City Planner did not object to the proposal on planning grounds, but Nardine's application was rejected by the Town Planning Committee as a result of residents' protests. Councillor Jack Marks supported Nardine's position, requesting others to 'act charitably', but the majority of councillors were opposed.[87] Nardine was again informed that a refuge was 'contrary to the orderly and proper planning of the locality, by virtue of increased traffic and disturbances on surrounding residential properties'.[88] Another appeal to the Minister for Planning, Pam Beggs, was upheld, the minister stating that

> there is a special case in support of your group being allowed to proceed with the use proposed for a period sufficient to enable the new refuge under construction…to be completed…I was particularly conscious of the service your group provides, the need to ensure that there is no break in the provision of this service, the undertakings your group has given on the way in which it will

conduct its activities, the suitability of the building on the site for the purpose, and the fact that it will only be necessary to conduct the refuge at this location during the period the new refuge…is being built.[89]

After what must have seemed like endless obstacles, and with some invaluable support, Nardine moved to the Berwick Street house in mid-1989 before finally relocating to the new refuge in 1991.

At the beginning of the 1980s, refuges had been 'a very lonely voice', but by the end of the decade, government was naming domestic violence and was beginning to take action. In 1990, the Department for Community Services reported that 'domestic violence continued to be a significant focus' of its work.[90] Nardine, in conjunction with other Western Australian refuges and the Women's Refuge Group, had relentlessly informed and challenged both government and the broader community about the existence of domestic violence and the need for services for women and children affected by it.

The history of the politicization of domestic violence in Western Australia demonstrates that the 'patriarchal state' was neither monolithic nor undifferentiated. The relationship between refuges and bureaucrats was variable: at times and in certain places, difficult; at others, productive. Substantial change did occur over these years, albeit painfully slowly for those working with the effects of domestic violence and for the women and children experiencing it.

# CHAPTER — 6

# A police station, a post office and a women's refuge: Responses to domestic violence in the 1990s

*The WA Government's response to domestic violence is recognised nationally for its innovation and breadth of strategies.*
WOMEN'S POLICY DEVELOPMENT OFFICE, 1999[1]

During the 1990s there was an unprecedented level of action taken in response to domestic violence. From the late 1980s, in the wake of the Western Australian Government's Domestic Violence Task Force, significant changes had begun. The initiatives of the 1990s built on these earlier programs. However, with a change of State Government in 1993, there was a new approach and revised directions. While a commitment to social change in relation to domestic violence was still evident, the orientation of these processes shifted. Increasingly in the 1990s, attention was drawn to reducing the incidence of domestic violence through perpetrator programs, and the Western Australian Liberal government put in place the ten-year 'Freedom from Fear' Campaign Against Domestic Violence. In addition, there continued to be intervention at Commonwealth level, with directions modified as a result of a change of government federally in 1996.

Despite this greater government activity, there has also been some concern that responses to domestic violence have become institutionalized. Refuges have become, as Pat Giles asserted, 'part of community expectations: you have a police station, you have a post office and you have a women's refuge'.[2] While this is clearly a positive development because it ensures that women and children are much more likely to have access to safe and supportive crisis accommodation and assistance, it also suggests that domestic violence is just another 'social evil' that has been identified, to which human services respond. This raises several questions. Is providing refuges enough? If more is done, will the resources available for services to women and children be reduced accordingly? And if there really is a commitment to social change and the prevention of domestic violence, are programs focusing on individual change rather than, or in addition to, structural change the most effective in the long term?

## KEEPING DOMESTIC VIOLENCE POLITICAL: THE FEDERAL LEVEL

The Labor Federal Government's National Committee on Violence Against Women ran for three years from 1990, with State and Commonwealth government and non-government representation. Its focus was domestic violence as well as other forms of violence against women, and it was directed towards policy development, research and community education. The committee's framework, as outlined in the *National Strategy on Violence Against Women*, took a radical feminist approach, suggesting that those working in women's refuges and sexual assault services had had a significant impact on the ways in which violence against women was understood. It specifically identified 'male violence' against women, including sexual assault, domestic violence and sexual harassment, as a continuum through which men exercised power. Male violence against women was defined as

> behaviour adopted to control the victim which results in physical, sexual and or psychological damage, forced social isolation or economic deprivation or behaviour which causes women to live in fear.[3]

This behaviour was seen to occur within a context of unequal gender power relations. It was noted that

> it is now being accepted that male violence arises from certain male attitudes, beliefs and behaviours in relation to women and

the abuse of power…Striving for the empowerment of women arises from the belief that violence against women has its origins in the social system which assigns subordinate status to women and that the origins of violence against women do not lie within individuals or relationships.[4]

Thus, the elimination of violence would require improvements in the status of women, including those concerned with women's access to economic independence, health and education.

Furthermore, other strategies were supported, including education at primary and secondary school levels to teach children about the links between violence and notions of masculinity, superiority and unequal rights; wider community education promoting the understanding that violence against women is a crime; and education of doctors, lawyers, magistrates, teachers and others on the effects of male violence.[5] In 1995, the Office of the Status of Women commissioned research to assess community attitudes to violence against women,[6] and in 1996 it produced the comic-style booklet *Violence at Home: The Big Secret*. Targeting young people, the booklet addressed issues such as understandings of masculinity and femininity and their relationship to violence, the impact of violence on children, and mechanisms of power and control in domestic violence, and included sources of help.[7]

The Labor government also made contributions internationally, recognizing violence against women as a violation of human rights, and building on the work done in the 1980s through the Convention on the Elimination of All Forms of Discrimination Against Women. In 1993, the United Nations' General Assembly unanimously passed the Declaration on the Elimination of Violence Against Women developed by the convention committee, chaired by former Chief Justice of the Australian Family Court Elizabeth Evatt. The declaration, while not having the force of a convention, nor signatories, does have international endorsement. It states that

violence against women is a manifestation of historically unequal power relations between men and women, which have led to domination over and discrimination against women by men and to the prevention of the full advancement of women, and…violence against women is one of the crucial social mechanisms by which women are forced into a subordinate position compared with men.[8]

Here, too, domestic violence was understood as a manifestation of gendered structural power inequalities.

In 1996, there was a change of government federally. Paul Keating's Labor government was replaced by a Liberal–National Party coalition led by John Howard. Domestic violence was also on the conservative parties' political agenda, and within a year of taking office Howard called together the National Domestic Violence Summit. Acknowledging the history of responses to domestic violence over the previous two decades, the Statement of Principles agreed to by Australian heads of government at the summit identified, among other matters, the 'context' of domestic violence:

Children often witness domestic violence and are profoundly affected by this experience.

Domestic violence is an abuse of power perpetrated mainly (but not only) by men against women both in a relationship and after separation.

Domestic violence takes a number of forms, both physical and psychological. The commonly acknowledged forms of domestic violence are physical and sexual violence, emotional and social abuse and economic deprivation.[9]

The Howard government's response to domestic violence was Partnerships Against Domestic Violence—a program involving the Commonwealth, States and Territories that was originally set up to run for three years (to 2001) and has since been extended. The Partnerships program is concerned with 'working together towards the common goal of preventing domestic violence and creating an Australian culture which is free from violence'.[10] Research and project development are the key strategies, and more than $25 million was allocated to this work over the three-year period 1997–2001. In the 1999–2000 budget, the government committed a further $25 million over four years (to 2003), through the Partnerships program, to the four priority areas of community education, work with perpetrators, Indigenous family violence and children at risk.[11]

The program has funded national initiatives such as the development of competency standards for workers with those affected by domestic violence, and the Australian Domestic and Family Violence Clearinghouse based at the University of New South Wales. It has also supported State-based research, including, in Western Australia, a pilot project developing counselling models for Indigenous men responsible for family violence, and additional funding to regional domestic violence committees to improve services to people from culturally and linguistically diverse backgrounds.

Australian social work academics Wendy Weeks and Lee FitzRoy have argued that there was a distinctly conservative turn in the politics of domestic violence during the late 1990s, which was in sharp contrast to the move towards radical feminist understandings in the earlier part of the decade. For example, the term 'violence against women', with its implied understanding that the various forms of violence against women are linked by unequal gender power relations, has been partly replaced by 'family violence'. While more inclusive of violence in Indigenous communities, the term 'family violence' no longer has a focus on women and sometimes includes child abuse and maltreatment. The need to 'help' violent men has become increasingly important, threatening the focus on women's safety and the criminalization of violence. These indicate a concern, once again, with keeping families together at any cost and contribute to the notion that domestic violence is not a gendered issue.[12]

In 2001, the Office of the Status of Women announced as a 'goal area' the 'elimination of violence in the lives of women'.[13] However, the work done through the Partnerships program in relation to domestic violence is not, as yet, directly linked to the new National Initiative to Combat Sexual Assault. While domestic violence has been identified as 'gendered violence', the various forms of violence against women have not been linked as manifestations of gendered structural power differences.[14]

The conservative political turn in understanding domestic violence was replicated at the Western Australian State level, also linked to a change of government in the early 1990s.

## RESPONSES AT THE STATE LEVEL

Domestic violence also stayed on the political agenda of the Western Australian State Governments during the 1990s. From 1987 to 1990, the Domestic Violence Coordinating Committee carried on the work of the Domestic Violence Task Force. In the committee's final report, it recommended ongoing across-government coordination of services concerning domestic violence and that a Domestic Violence Policy and Research Branch be established in the Office of the Family. This unit would be responsible for conducting research, formulating and reviewing policy and legislation across government related to domestic violence, analysing training needs and facilitating the development of training, developing community education campaigns and providing community funding, with the aim of addressing and preventing domestic violence. The establishment of an area of government identifiably devoted to domestic violence policy and program development was a significant step, even though the unit had a monumental mandate and limited resources.

In 1990, the Domestic Violence Coordinating Committee was replaced by the Domestic Violence Advisory Council. The council included representatives of government and community organizations and was chaired by Labor Member of the Legislative Assembly Dr Judy Edwards. It provided community input into government planning for domestic violence service provision and law reform.

In 1992, the Western Australian Labor government produced a report detailing future directions of its responses to domestic violence and proposed mechanisms to prevent the incidence of domestic violence. First, it gave some indication of changes that had occurred:

Over the past ten years the Western Australian Government and community have been working together to assist women and children who are the victims of domestic violence to obtain protection and support. Because our community has only recently begun to act on the issue of domestic violence, our response so far has focussed on the provision of immediate crisis assistance, but this, whilst certainly crucial, is not enough. Our aim must be no less than the elimination of violence in the home.[15]

In particular, it was noted that there had been increased community awareness of domestic violence and that improved responses had resulted from training across agencies and professions.[16] The government proposed a range of approaches to the further improvement of responses to domestic violence and to its prevention and reduction. Both educational and legislative means were suggested as ways of prevention. For example, a Domestic Violence and Child Abuse Prevention Education Program was developed as part of the K-10 Health Syllabus in Western Australian State schools, with the aim of enhancing 'young people's capacity to participate in non-violent relationships'.[17] It was based on the assumption that

[i]f domestic violence is to be prevented, everyone should receive education on domestic violence, and all school aged children should be assisted to develop skills which will enable them to form healthy adult relationships based on assertiveness, communication, sensitivity and respect for the rights of others.[18]

On the advice of the Domestic Violence Advisory Council, the Labor government was also pursuing specific domestic violence legislation:

The Government will introduce domestic violence legislation into Parliament which will ensure the immediate protection of the victims of violence in the home. It will also stand as a statement from the whole community to those who might be violent that domestic violence will not be tolerated. It is clear that domestic violence will not be eliminated until the community as a whole commits itself to the task: the legislation will emphasize the criminal nature of domestic violence and be a focal point for public condemnation of domestic violence.[19]

With the change of State Government in 1993, domestic violence legislation was not pursued. In the new Liberal–National coalition government, Roger Nicholls, MLC, became the Minister for Community Development, heading the government department with considerable responsibility for domestic violence issues. The Department for Community Development (formerly Community Services), under the previous Labor government, had taken on the across-government coordination role in relation to domestic violence and was involved in policy and program development. Under Nicholls's ministerial leadership, and later during the 1990s under Rhonda Parker and then June van de Klashorst, further changes were to occur, indicating new directions in relation to domestic violence.

The change in direction was almost immediately evident. In 1994, the Department for Community Development (soon to become Family and Children's Services, reflecting a change in orientation) published a document outlining 'a campaign aimed at reducing the incidence of abuse in families'. The 'Abuse in Families' campaign included the Family Helpline telephone counselling service and mass media advertising. A 'conservative turn' was evident in the focus of the campaign. It included both child abuse and 'spouse abuse' (not 'domestic violence'), and 'spouse abuse' was ungendered and unrelated to other forms of violence against women, even though it was acknowledged in market research that the community understood men to be the primary perpetrators and women and children the victims.[20] The background information document to the campaign called on families and communities to take responsibility for the abuse:

Family members have a responsibility to protect themselves and other family members from all forms of abuse including child emotional, physical and sexual abuse and neglect; and spouse abuse. The responsibility to prevent these forms of abuse cannot be taken solely by the Government, but must involve action by families to help themselves, and by community members to help prevent abuse.[21]

Only after calling to attention the responsibilities of the 'family' and the community to protect themselves and prevent abuse does the document find its way to those who perpetrate the abuse, but still it does not identify them: 'In addition, those who abuse other family members need to accept full responsibility for their actions'.[22]

The conservative political turn could also be seen in the way in which the Family Helpline's activities were discussed in the 1996–97 Annual Report of Family and Children's Services. The Family Helpline was described as 'a telephone counselling and information service for families experiencing relationship difficulties'; 75 per cent of more than 9,500 calls were made by women, and 18 per cent were related to 'marital/de facto relationship problem' and 4 per cent to 'spouse abuse'. During the same period, Crisis Care received 41,700 calls, of which 9.2 per cent were related to 'domestic violence' and 19 per cent to 'relationship issues'.[23]

Further evidence of more conservative understandings of domestic violence is found in the 2000 Family and Children's Services *Domestic Violence Policy*. Here, domestic violence is defined as 'an extreme form of family conflict'. At the same time, it is described as 'any abusive behaviour by one partner in a relationship to gain and maintain control over another'.[24]

The 'Abuse in Families' campaign was superseded in 1995, when, with a change of minister, the Western Australian Government's Family and Domestic Violence Task Force, chaired by Liberal Member of the Legislative Assembly June van de Klashorst, produced the Family and Domestic Violence Action Plan aimed at preventing and reducing the incidence of domestic and family violence. It highlighted the need to:

- maintain and improve services and support to all victims;
- place a greater emphasis on programs and perpetrators and potential perpetrators;

- change community attitudes through a long term community education campaign; and,
- build on existing structures and encourage 'grass roots' partnerships.[25]

There were several notable outcomes from the Action Plan. First was the establishment in 1996 of the Crime and Domestic Violence Transitional Unit, located in the Department of Premier and Cabinet, later to be named the Domestic Violence Prevention Unit and moved to the Women's Policy Development Office (in 1999, renamed the Women's Policy Office). While the Women's Policy Office is concerned with women, the Domestic Violence Prevention Unit has a wider mandate, including men, women and children. Its positioning, however, to some extent, works against the belief that domestic violence is more than a 'women's issue', and that coordinated and collaborative across-government approaches are needed, although the Women's Policy Office is also concerned with 'coordinated and collaborative across-government approaches' to improving the status of women. Despite this rather incongruous positioning, Carole Kagi, the director of the Domestic Violence Prevention Unit, argued that the Action Plan does have 'teeth'. She asserted, for example, that the Action Plan and the work of the unit were strongly supported by the two Liberal ministers who held the portfolio, that the Action Plan was endorsed by Cabinet, and that it has been monitored through the Justice Coordinating Committee, a subcommittee of Cabinet and chaired by the Attorney General.[26] In 2002, the positioning and activities of the Domestic Violence Prevention Unit are being reviewed.

Second, domestic violence regional committees were established in the sixteen police regions across Western Australia, with the task of implementing the Action Plan. The regional committees developed their own regional plans, and 'victim and perpetrator services were identified as integral to the implementation of these plans'.[27] The regional committees comprised government officers and others with expertise in the field of domestic violence, including refuge workers. Lois Gatley, who was involved in the initial development of the regional committees, observed the way that these people with commit-ment worked together:

> I saw it in practice where relationships got built between people who had never sat at the same table, never really listened to each other before. Homeswest was a classic example of this and where some things got put in place because of that relationship. Refuge workers, who were good at negotiating and at building relation-ships, got people on side and won people over, won over police, won over other people who in the past had seen them as people not to talk to.[28]

The regional committee structure put in place mechanisms for the planning of work in relation to domestic violence at a regional level and for this work to be done in a collaborative and coordinated manner. However, there have been concerns that the regional committees have been under-resourced.

A third outcome of the Action Plan has been the establishment of 'best practice' guidelines for working with both victims and perpetra-tors. They are an attempt to

> collect and collate all the existing knowledge and expertise within both community organisations and government agencies to ensure that consistent standards of service are offered to victims of family and domestic violence in the future.[29]

As indicators of social change, the 'best practice' documents suggest, at policy level at least, an incorporation of feminist ideas about domestic violence. Their development included the work of those who have had a long-term commitment to providing high-quality services to women and children experiencing domestic violence. While the 'best practice' documents were not intended for refuge workers but rather those in generalist services, they recognized that they had invaluable experience and knowledge and drew on their expertise in informing others in the wider domestic violence field.[30]

Other outcomes of the Action Plan have been the 'Freedom from Fear' Campaign Against Domestic Violence and the planned Aboriginal Family Violence Strategy, discussed below.

Women's refuges and others working with domestic violence had high hopes that the Labor government, newly elected in 2001, would fulfil its policies concerning domestic violence services. The Labor Party platform included increased funding to domestic violence regional committees, women's refuges, outreach services, children's counselling and the Women's Refuge Group; establishment of a twenty-four hour helpline for victims of domestic violence; and a review of the need for specific domestic violence legislation. Since the change of government, funding has been allocated to some of these initiatives.[31]

## FAMILY VIOLENCE AND INDIGENOUS WOMEN AND CHILDREN

As noted previously, Indigenous people have tended to prefer the term 'family violence' to 'domestic violence', to acknowledge the ways in which violence affects a range of family members, not just women and children.[32] In the 1990s, the needs of Indigenous women and children in relation to domestic violence were increasingly highlighted. It has become apparent that Indigenous women and children experience family violence at much higher rates than non-Indigenous women and that human service responses must better recognize their needs, interests and concerns.[33] Research undertaken by the Crime Research Centre at The University of Western Australia in 1995 found:

- 90% of reported domestic violence victims are women and more than half are Aboriginal;
- Aboriginal people (overwhelmingly women) are, according to police recorded victimisation rates, 53 times more likely to be a victim of domestic violence than non-Aboriginal people;

- Aboriginal victims sustain more serious injuries than non-Aboriginal victims and require more hospitalisation; and,
- More than half of reported domestic violence cases occur outside Perth.[34]

The greater recognition of the extent and severity of domestic violence among Indigenous women has led to the development of more appropriate services and programs. During the 1990s, SAAP and other funding was made available to establish services that targeted Indigenous women, children and families. For example, the Derby Family Healing Centre is an accommodation and support service that operates on a 'family healing' model. It attempts to reduce family violence rather than assist women to leave their violent partners. An Indigenous family violence outreach service was established in Coolbellup, funded by the Department of Family and Children's Services. The Partnerships Against Domestic Violence program includes research targeting Indigenous people, such as the development of service provision models for Indigenous men who have perpetrated violence, and the national Indigenous family violence community awareness program, 'Walking into Doors', featuring Indigenous musicians Ruby Hunter and Archie Roach.[35]

The proposed Western Australian Aboriginal Family Violence Strategy focuses on capacity building at a local level, aims to increase respect for Indigenous culture, and builds partnerships between the Indigenous community and government services. Taking the 'whole healing approach' as outlined by the Aboriginal Justice Council for the Family and Domestic Violence Task Force, the proposed strategy argues that

> a simple patriarchal interpretation of Aboriginal family violence is inadequate and sanctioning the perpetrator through means of the criminal justice system alone leads to further destruction of Aboriginal society and culture...family violence should be seen as a broad based community problem which demands a community services response not a narrow criminal justice response.[36]

As further outlined in the proposed strategy, significant change is required to the ways that legal services, police, courts, correctional services, women's refuges, and counselling and other support services currently respond to Indigenous people.

Clearly, the healing approach taken by some Indigenous people is in contrast to the radical feminist model that focuses more on putting in place mechanisms for women's and children's safety by their removal from the male perpetrator of violence. It also challenges feminist understandings by emphasizing the destructive effects of racism and colonialism over patriarchy.

## THE SUPPORTED ACCOMMODATION ASSISTANCE PROGRAM AND REFUGE FUNDING

In the 1990s, SAAP continued to fund women's refuges, as well as youth, family and single men's services. In contrast to SAAP mark I (1985–89), where the focus was on the provision of crisis accommodation services and the problem was identified within SAAP as homelessness (even though refuges clearly thought otherwise), SAAP mark II (1989–94) focused on 'transitional accommodation', with greater emphasis placed on support services. (Refuges like Nardine had, since their commencement, articulated *supported* crisis accommodation as central to their service delivery.) SAAP mark III (1994–99) worked towards individualization of client services through the introduction of case management and service standards, and attempted to measure performance through national data collections. SAAP mark IV, in effect from 2000 to 2005, aims to continue a focus on client-centred service delivery and to maintain support for homeless people that promotes independence and self-reliance.[37]

In 2001, SAAP provided funding to thirty-four women's refuges and six domestic violence outreach services. The annual funding of these services for that year was over $11 million.[38]

As noted, SAAP III had a greater concern with 'quality and measurement' promoted through the introduction of service standards, case management and national data collections.[39] While the service standards had been developed through SAAP earlier in the 1990s, they were not implemented until 1998. The tender to undertake this work was won by the Women's Refuge Group and the project was carried out by Lois Gatley and her co-workers Fay Sambo and Violet Pickett. During the process, which Gatley stressed was a developmental one, the field had the opportunity to reflect further on the standards and to highlight gaps, particularly concerning the needs of children. According to Gatley, further work was required to resource agencies to assist them to meet service standards.

In 1998, case management was introduced and promoted to refuges, to ensure greater attention to and follow up of the needs of individual women. From around this time, greater attention was also being paid to case management of children in refuges, recognizing that they have needs separate and in addition to those of their mothers. The provision of counselling for these children is part of this process.

Also in 1998 was the introduction of the first industrial award for Western Australian refuge workers. The CASH Award requires the payment of refuge workers to recognized standards. An outcome of this, as noted by Kedy Kristal, has been 'a very strong push towards people having recognised qualifications now whereas at Nardine [in the earlier years] not having qualifications was more likely to get you a job'.[40]

Nardine was already paying workers at a level largely consistent with the CASH Award for their experience and qualifications, whereas in some other refuges the award resulted in significant salary increases. Because of the refuge's history of being a collective, the pooled funds at Nardine had been shared among workers, and all received the same level of pay. There was not a hierarchical structure, requiring different levels of payment, until 1998. With the appointment of a coordinator (Level 7), an outreach worker position (Level 5) and incremental steps within the refuge worker positions at Level 4, more funding was required to top up Nardine's salaries budget. SAAP considered increases in funding to implement the CASH Award conditions on a case-by-case basis. Some additional funding was forthcoming, but in 2002 there is insufficient funding to adequately support the developing outreach service. Nardine is now considering fund-raising strategies to support its work, though it is unlikely that the refuge's supporters will rattle tins in the Hay Street Mall again to pay workers' wages, as they did in the 1980s.

Increasingly during the 1990s, neo-liberal government policies and economic rationalism affected the community sector. For example, the underpinning assumption about the way that refuges (and other community organizations) were funded changed. In 1994, the 'Funding of Services model for the provision of funding to non-government organisations' was introduced:

> Under this model, the funding of services is determined using a needs based planning approach which takes into consideration current service provision and the need for further services in the context of the available budget and departmental priorities. New services are advertised seeking Requests for Proposals from interested organisations willing to provide the services. When funding services, the department must operate within the legislative and administrative requirements set down by the State Supply Commission and Contract and Management Services. There are specific policies to follow to determine the allocation of funds to services and the continuation of funding to existing service providers.[41]

An alternative way of understanding this model of funding community organizations is suggested by Kedy Kristal, a former Nardine worker and now manager of another women's refuge, the Patricia Giles Centre:

> The government through Family and Children's Services is purchasing a service from us that we are paid to supply. They dictate what they will and won't purchase. This is the complete flip side from the community development model of 'this is what we want to do to address this need, can we have some money?'

Thus, community organizations now compete for funding to establish new services in the same way that tenders are called for a range of non-welfare related services. In a political environment of economic rationalism, this raises a number of concerns, such as whether the organization that puts in the lowest bid or the one best able to meet the identified needs 'wins' the tender.[42] Large, generic welfare organizations might be more likely to 'win' tenders for new domestic violence services because of the economies of scale offered by their operations. Others argue that although small community-based feminist organizations might have difficulty competing economically, they have greater understanding of and expertise in the area of domestic violence.

Initially, when this new model was introduced by the then Minister for Family and Children's Services, Roger Nicholls, it was proposed that all services, including existing services such as Nardine that had been in operation for more than twenty years, would have to compete with others in their region (in Nardine's case, another long-established refuge, Mary Smith Refuge) for ongoing government funding. After considerable public opposition, however, the government relented and moved to a 'Preferred Provider' model. Established services such as Nardine retained their funding, subject to ongoing departmental monitoring.

## WORKING WITH PERPETRATORS AND PREVENTING DOMESTIC VIOLENCE

The focus in this book is on women and children escaping domestic violence rather than on those who perpetrate the violence. This is not surprising. Until relatively recently, there has been little done to deal systematically with perpetrators other than the limited and seemingly inconsistently applied criminal justice response. Over the 1990s, however, responses to domestic violence widened to include both mandatory and voluntary programs that attempted to change men's behaviour.

Strategies attempting to prevent domestic violence or to work with perpetrators to change their behaviour were identified as being potentially contentious. The 1997 Annual Report of the Western Australian Government's Women's Policy Development Office stated that it is pertinent to comment on initiatives amongst our domestic violence responsibilities that will actually provide services for men. The purists might argue that we should not concern ourselves with men, but we take the view that we must think bigger and tackle the difficult and insidious problem of domestic violence from several angles at once.[43]

Despite the suggestion that (radical feminist) 'purists' did not agree, the women interviewed for this book noted work with men as a necessary part of the process of social change in relation to domestic violence. However, among those who support the need 'to tackle the difficult and insidious problem of domestic violence from several angles at once', there is blanket agreement that services to women and children must not be jeopardized or reduced because of the demands of providing services to perpetrators.

Many women who have experienced domestic violence say that they do not want the relationship to end but rather the violence to stop. Former Nardine worker Glenda Blake has argued that if 'that's what women are saying they want [perpetrator programs] [then] I think that it's important to listen'.[44]

Another long-term worker in domestic violence services, Maureen Hatton, is also an advocate of the need to work with men as well as women. She passionately believes that a criminal justice intervention model and inter-agency collaboration are

essential elements to ending violence against women. One of the main reasons for becoming involved with the model was to promote community responsibility. After twenty-five years, refuges were witnessing the revolving door. Women kept returning, young women who had been residents as children were coming in with their children and refuge workers appeared to be the only ones ensuring women's safety. It became apparent that until and unless offenders are made accountable and responsible for their behaviour the violence would never end and we would have to keep building more refuges.[45]

As outreach worker at Starick House women's refuge, Hatton was involved in piloting the first domestic violence criminal justice intervention project in Western Australia during the early 1990s. The project, known as the Armadale Domestic Violence Intervention Project, was an initiative of the Domestic Violence Action Groups of Western Australia (now named the Domestic Violence Council); the Domestic Violence Action Groups were local community organizations that lobbied for social change in relation to domestic violence. The Armadale project was based on models from Hamilton, New Zealand, and Duluth, United States. Hatton noted that at this time, the project received little support from government. The primary support came from the Armadale Police and, in particular, the officer-in-charge, Sergeant Fred Heald, with involvement from local government and other non-government community organizations. It was not until 1996 that the Armadale project received ongoing government funding.

Others working in the field from the early 1990s included Dawson Ruhl and Ros Adam at Relationships Australia in Fremantle. Ruhl ran Western Australia's first domestic violence mandated offenders' program, Adam ran a women's group, and counselling in relation to domestic violence was available to both men and women. The domestic violence offenders' program involved a twenty-six week course that 'challenged patriarchal assumptions, promoted the concept of equality in relationships and placed the locus of responsibility for the violence with the perpetrator'.[46]

In the late 1990s, the 'Freedom from Fear' Campaign Against Domestic Violence was the main plank of the Western Australian Government's approach to preventing domestic violence. Started in 1998 under the Court Liberal government, 'Freedom from Fear' is a ten-year 'innovative social marketing initiative' with associated support strategies. While arguing that the incarceration of violent men is a necessary aspect of domestic violence prevention, the developers of this campaign claim that the fear of the perpetrator remains, even after incarceration. Furthermore, as noted above, 'many women do not want to leave the relationship, nor do they want the man incarcerated; they simply want the violence to stop'.[47] Thus, 'Freedom from Fear' aims 'to reduce the fears of women (and children) by motivating perpetrators and potential perpetrators to *voluntarily* attend counselling programs' (italics in original).[48] The campaign 'reaches out to perpetrators rather than victims' and aims to 'change the behaviour and attitudes of abusive men'.[49] In further justifying the underpinning rationale for the 'Freedom from Fear' campaign, Carole Kagi, the director of the Domestic Violence Prevention Unit where the campaign is located, explained:

> We know that very few people go to the police…So very few people are going to go through the criminal justice system. Obviously we've got to work on improving that but if only a small number are going to get into programs through the criminal justice system as mandated offenders, we have a large group out there that we have got to reach through any other means. And that's where the Campaign comes in and a whole range of other strategies to access those people affected by domestic violence…We're saying we need to do things in a variety of ways to reach as many people as possible.

Kagi's comments raise the issue of the extent to which domestic violence is a crime. While sexual and physical violence are clearly criminal acts, other forms of domestic violence are not. As Kagi noted:

> [T]he law does not cover economic deprivation or social isolation or psychological abuse. They're not currently criminal offences so they're not going to get a response out of the police and the criminal justice system on that.

The 'Freedom from Fear' campaign uses mass media advertising to create awareness of the Men's Domestic Violence Helpline, targeting 'violent' and 'potentially violent' men. In the first three years (September 1999 to June 2001), more than 9,500 calls were received. A large proportion (65 per cent) of those calling were men in the campaign's primary target group, and more than 4,000 (42 per cent) were self-identified as such. Approximately half (48 per cent) of these men

(1,950) accepted a voluntary referral into men's behaviour change programs.[50]

The Men's Domestic Violence Helpline attracted many more calls than were expected. Carole Kagi remarked:

> [F]irstly, we didn't think that men would ring up and identify that they were responsible for domestic violence, and secondly, that they would give identifying details and accept referral to a behaviour change program.

While little is known about the effectiveness of voluntary and mandated programs, a research project funded by Partnerships Against Domestic Violence is reviewing the evaluation tools of such programs and assessing the effectiveness of perpetrator programs across Western Australia.[51] One concern in relation to voluntary programs is that while men will accept referrals, they do not necessarily persevere. For example, a man might enter a voluntary program while experiencing the remorse stage of the cycle of violence but withdraw when either things get too difficult or the woman returns to the relationship.[52] There have also been reported concerns regarding adherence to best practice by agencies running intervention programs, in relation to maintaining women's safety.[53]

Productive relationships have been established between those in services for women and children in the domestic violence field and those in government, but there have also been ongoing tensions. The 'Freedom from Fear' campaign has been a site of some of these tensions, at least partly because of the concern that it is a reorientation away from radical feminist understandings of domestic violence and that it directs funds away from services for women and children. While some argue that men, women and children do benefit from 'Freedom from Fear', others assert that its effectiveness is limited and that its underlying philosophy is problematic. First, the campaign aims only to produce individual behaviour change rather than systemic structural change. It is not linked to the wider issue of violence against women, nor is this understood as a manifestation of gender inequity. While perpetrators are made aware of the inequity in power within their own relationships, these programs do not challenge the power imbalances at a societal level that exist and that are (potentially) manifested as domestic violence in intimate relationships. Clearly, this goal would require a very different approach. However, it could be argued that other (liberal feminist) government strategies are attempting to achieve change to improve the status of women—for example, programs that attempt to modify the sexual division of labour and increase women's economic independence. Another strategy is the promotion of women's participation in executive decision-making. Despite these efforts, however, in 1999 women received only 76.6 per cent of men's full-time adult ordinary earnings and formed only 1.3 per cent of executive directors of Australasian boards.[54]

A second concern with the campaign is that advertisements are concerned specifically with the impact of domestic violence on children rather than on women. However, research undertaken to inform the development of the campaign found that

> the most effective motivating theme for those accepting of their need to change was *the consequence of the perpetrator's behaviour on children*.[55] [italics in original]

'Damage to partner' was believed unlikely to motivate change by both those identified as 'perpetrators' and other 'men in the general community' who participated in focus groups to consider what would be a successful theme for a domestic violence prevention campaign. Instead, 'damage to children' was seen as universally effective. Among those who participated in this phase of the market research, strong feelings were expressed for their children; there was awareness of their children's responses to specific incidences of violence; and some revealed their own feelings about having been affected by domestic violence as children.[56]

While the campaign makes use of what was found to be the most effective strategy to promote the message that domestic violence is unacceptable, it also suggests and confirms some men's beliefs that

every time you hurt her

he feels it too

MEN'S HELPLINE
1800 000 599

Poster image depicting the impact of domestic violence on children, from the 'Freedom from Fear' Campaign Against Domestic Violence, 1998.
*Courtesy Domestic Violence Prevention Unit, Women's Policy Office, Government of Western Australia*

'damage to partner' is less important. However, those taking a pragmatic approach argue that we should use whatever approaches are necessary to prevent and reduce the incidence of domestic violence, regardless of suggested implications concerning the importance of women.

Finally, there is also a concern in relation to the relative resourcing of programs for men, women and children. Why, some ask, do 'violent' and 'potentially violent' men get free professional counselling to help them change their behaviour, when women and children have what is considered to be limited access to free professional counselling services to deal with the effects of this behaviour? While significant amounts of money go into refuge services for women and children, these services do not typically provide professional counselling but rather other forms of support, advocacy and crisis accommodation. In response to these concerns, the Domestic Violence Prevention Unit has asserted that victim counselling services are provided by Family and Children's Services (from 2001, renamed the Department for Community Development), the Ministry of Justice and the Crisis Care Unit and that these add up to more than the funding dedicated to perpetrator counselling services.[57]

Related to concerns about the relative resourcing of men's and women's programs is the way that 'Freedom from Fear' raises the issue of domestic violence not only for men but for women and children. As noted above, around 65 per cent of calls to the Men's Domestic Violence Helpline have been from men in the target group. According to statistics collected by the Domestic Violence Prevention Unit, since the campaign began in 1998 an average of 13 per cent of calls—up to 18 per cent more recently—have been from women who are victims of domestic violence.[58] It would not be surprising, then, if there was an increase in demand for support services for women and children as a result of the campaign. While some additional funding has been made available for these purposes, this response also suggests the need for a dedicated helpline for women and children seeking assistance in relation to domestic violence.

Over the 1990s, refuges became institutionalized in the social landscape, but there were also attempts to eliminate the need for them. Services for perpetrators were developed, in an attempt to prevent further domestic violence. Feminists debated the effectiveness of largely individualized responses that did not take into account the impact of patriarchal social structures. As the concerns of Indigenous people began to be heard more clearly, some approaches challenged radical feminist responses to domestic violence by focusing on family healing.

While human services' understandings of domestic violence and their responses to it have clearly changed significantly since 1974, many issues remain. In 2002, policing continues to be an issue of concern, despite the supportive position of the Police Commissioner, Barry

Western Australian Police Commissioner Barry Matthews shows his support for action against domestic violence, at the Women's Refuge Group breakfast, April 2000. Here with Liberal Member of the Legislative Council Barbara Scott and Soroptimist International spokeswoman Lynley Lord, he looks at a quilt honouring women and children who have died as a result of domestic violence. *West Australian*, 29 April 2000, p. 12. *Courtesy* West Australian

Matthews, that 'police must treat domestic violence as a crime and aggressively prosecute offenders'.[59] Public housing is virtually unattainable and typically requires long periods on a so-called 'priority' waiting list. General practitioners and other health care providers need to be further educated about the nature and effects of domestic violence and the available support services. Domestic violence against people with disabilities has yet to be addressed in any systematic manner.[60] Homicides as a result of domestic violence continue to occur with shocking frequency, and the needs of children who are affected by domestic violence require further action.

Feminists are seeking change around all these issues. For example, the Women's Refuge Group continues to lobby for changes to Ministry of Housing policies and practices and an increase in the available public housing stock. Refuge staff work with police recruits and officers to inform them about domestic violence and its effects. And every year since 1990, domestic violence memorial marches have been held to honour and remember the women and children who have died as a result of domestic violence.

# Conclusion: Doing themselves out of a job?

> When I look back over the last twenty-five years, I sometimes think that
> it is three steps forward and two steps backwards...
> LOIS GATLEY, 2000[1]

In the 1970s, the goal of feminist refuges around Australia was to eliminate domestic violence. As Deborah Dearnley recalled, refuge philosophy in the early days was 'to do ourselves out of a job'.[2] While this has
not been achieved, other, practical changes have occurred. In 1974,
hundreds of women and children were turned away from the four existing refuges in Perth. Refuges were stretched and there was nowhere else
for women to turn. In 2002, there are forty women's refuges and outreach services that assist women and children throughout Western Australia, and if they are all full, or if a woman is not within travelling
distance of a service, the Department for Community Development
pays for temporary accommodation at a motel. Women and children
no longer sleep on mattresses on the floor. Refuges have standards for
service delivery that impose a maximum number of families that can be
accommodated at any refuge.

In economic terms, funding for domestic violence services has
also changed significantly. In 1974, donations of 50 cents per week
from Perth's feminists and their supporters kept Nardine afloat, and
there were no government funds identified for domestic violence services. In 2001, the Department for Community Development, the
Western Australian Government department with the greatest identified commitment to the issue of domestic violence, allocated over

$12 million to non-government domestic violence services, of which $10 million was for crisis accommodation.[3] A fifth of all funding to non-government services provided by the Department for Community Development targets domestic violence.[4] In addition, since 1997 the Federal Government has committed $50 million to the Partnerships Against Domestic Violence initiative. But as Kedy Kristal argues, while there is more money, there are also more players.[5] No longer are women's refuges the only ones in the domestic violence field. Funds are now allocated to prevention programs that target men, and counselling is provided to attempt to change men's violent behaviour.

For these changes in funding and in the practicalities of service provision to have occurred, domestic violence first had to be identified, named and defined. In 1974, the term 'domestic violence' was not used and there were only the beginnings of the development of a feminist conceptualization that captured women's experiences of 'intolerable domestic situations', building on that identified through Erin Pizzey's work in London from the early 1970s. The identification, naming and defining of domestic violence were significant steps in ensuring that responses were put in place to both support those affected by it and attempt to prevent it.

The desire of Nardine's workers and the Western Australian refuge movement to eliminate domestic violence has been espoused by others, as well. In 1990, Prime Minister Bob Hawke declared, through the National Agenda for Women, that 'by the year 2000…the Government hopes to see an Australia which is free from violence in the home…'.[6] Similarly, in 1992, the Western Australian Labor government stated that its 'aim must be no less than the elimination of violence in the home'.[7] More recently, the Howard Federal Government's response to domestic violence, Partnerships Against Domestic Violence, has been concerned with 'working together towards the common goal of preventing domestic violence and creating an Australian culture which is free from violence'.[8]

Clearly, then, there has been social change in relation to the identification of domestic violence as a social issue, the provision of services, and the political desire to eliminate, or at least to reduce, its incidence. But for all this allocation of resources, is there evidence of change in the incidence of domestic violence? This is a problematic question because there is no historical baseline. In addition, there have been changes over time of what is understood to constitute domestic violence. Because of the personal and private nature of the problem, we cannot say that in 1974 domestic violence occurred with any particular frequency, because most incidents were never reported. If its reported frequency has increased over time, this is due to changes in community perceptions about domestic violence. In 2002, it is more acceptable for women to tell others of their experiences and to seek assistance from the increasingly available services, and any increase in reported incidents might be a result of this, rather than because men are becoming more violent within their intimate relationships.

Based on Australian Bureau of Statistics information from the mid-1990s, it was estimated that a quarter of Australian women have experienced domestic violence.[9] Furthermore, some evidence of the prevalence of domestic violence may be found among requests for assistance to the Crisis Care Unit, the numbers of violence restraining orders issued and health workers' reports of women seeking treatment as a result of injuries caused by domestic violence. During the 1990s, approximately 10 per cent of calls to the Crisis Care Unit were identified as related to domestic violence. On average, more than 600 violence restraining orders were issued in Western Australia every month. In 1996–97, more than half of all homicides in the State were the result of a domestic violence incident.[10]

Hospitals and general practitioners are also commonly at the frontline of domestic violence responses. In research published in the *Medical Journal of Australia* during the 1990s, it was reported that 14 per cent of people attending hospital accident and emergency departments were there due to domestic violence; 22 per cent of women in a general practice setting had experienced physical violence in the previous year; and 30 per cent of women attending a hospital antenatal clinic during a one-month period had a history of experiencing domestic violence.[11]

The demographics of the population seeking assistance in relation to domestic violence may also be changing. For example, in 2000–01, Nardine provided accommodation to fifty-seven women and 102 children. (In addition, 136 women sought assistance from the outreach worker.) Of the women who stayed at the refuge, 42 per cent were Anglo-Australian, 30 per cent were Indigenous and 28 per cent were women from culturally and linguistically diverse backgrounds. The proportion of women from this last group has increased in recent times.[12]

All these statistics are indicators of an incidence of domestic violence that continues to be widespread and intolerably high. Despite changes in service provision that, according to South Australian researcher Dale Bagshaw and her colleagues, 'have had a positive impact on the experiences of women, men and children seeking help for domestic violence', there is still no evidence that domestic violence is being eliminated.[13]

While the use of services such as the Crisis Care Unit and women's refuges and the number of police requests are some guide to the prevalence of domestic violence, community perceptions are an indicator of the attitudes that promote or prevent it. Since the 1980s, several studies have been undertaken, and some change is apparent. Significantly, however, the belief that violence against women is warranted in some circumstances still persists.

The national domestic violence campaign community survey in 1987 revealed 'a disquieting level of community tolerance of violence by men against their wives'.[14] In 1995, the Office of the Status of Women recorded some change when it recommissioned research to assess community attitudes. On the basis of telephone interviews with more than 2,000 Australians, it found that

> there is much greater awareness and understanding of domestic violence than was the case eight years ago. It is clearly recognised as a problem, and is no longer a taboo subject in the community. The community now understands that domestic violence is *not* just physical violence; that it is a crime; that no sections of the community are immune; that it is *not* a private or hidden matter; that provocation is *not* justification for violence; and that alcohol is *not* an excuse...However, the community continues to be

judgemental of women who experience domestic violence and does not want to get involved'.[15] [emphasis in original]

Despite the apparent change in understanding concerning some aspects of domestic violence, other surveys indicated entrenched perceptions. A 1994 survey of Western Australian families found that 20 per cent of respondents believed that it was 'acceptable to use force against a woman in some circumstances'.[16] This outcome was replicated in the 1995 Office of the Status of Women research, which found that 18 per cent of respondents agreed that there were circumstances in which physical force by a husband against his wife was justifiable. In 1996, market research undertaken in the development of the Western Australian 'Freedom from Fear' Campaign Against Domestic Violence used focus groups comprising a range of Western Australian men. While appreciating that domestic violence was a 'very important issue which is firmly on the "social agenda"', and understanding that it included severe physical assault, there was limited recognition of the effects of the fear of physical assault, physical intimidation and threats, verbal abuse, social isolation, economic deprivation or sexual abuse.[17] In a 1999 study in which a group of Western Australian men were surveyed, nursing academic Anne McMurray and her colleagues found that 15 per cent believed that violence against women was justified, and a further 31 per cent thought that it was justified sometimes. Forty per cent of those interviewed believed that men's violence was provoked by a woman's behaviour.[18]

Acceptance of domestic violence is not confined to lay people. Within the medical and legal professions, for example, there are those who have limited understanding of domestic violence and its effects, and whose attitudes can have significant impact on the lives of women and children. Thus, we cannot assume that women's access to legal advice means that justice is served. In its inaugural report of 1996, the Domestic Violence Legal Unit of Legal Aid Western Australia reported that women 'may confront magistrates who are ignorant of the effects of domestic violence, lack empathy, or who are simply callous in their approach'.[19] Clients of the unit seeking restraining orders due to domestic violence came up against these concerns, as illustrated by the following examples:

> Client sought a restraining order because of a history of physical violence, bullying and threats by her husband. The woman was refused a hearing because the magistrate "'considered it a family law matter'". The DVLU took the case on appeal to the Supreme Court and was successful. The matter was then heard by a different magistrate and the order was granted for one year.[20]

> Client had an interim restraining order against her estranged husband. They had been married for many years; his violent and obsessive behaviour increased over time. The client had been assaulted just prior to the separation and there had been a number of breaches of the interim order. The order was granted for one year, but the magistrate commented that "'I think there is more to this than meets the eye'" and only granted the order because the husband had (in breach of the interim order) placed obscene signs about his wife in the local area.[21]

While acknowledging that there are magistrates who are 'handling [domestic violence] cases with sensitivity', there is 'the need for a more enlightened approach by magistrates'.[22] The 1994 Chief Justice's Taskforce on Gender Bias further elaborated on these concerns and attempted to set in place training for senior judiciary to inform them about domestic violence and its effects.[23]

Despite the work of a generation of feminist activists and their allies within parliament, government bureaucracies and elsewhere, there are still entrenched and insidious attitudes that reflect beliefs that women are inferior and deserving of violence, or that this behaviour is condoned in others. That these values remain gives credence to a radical feminist understanding of patriarchy and its effects. The wider society in which men dominate must also change before there is long-lasting and widespread change in relation to violence against women. This clearly would entail a transformation in social structures and conceptualizations of gender. How this could be achieved is uncertain. Some support stronger and better coordinated and integrated criminal justice responses. At the same time, continuing programs that tackle violence against women specifically, such as education campaigns and support services, as well as broader programs such as equal employment opportunity measures and family-friendly social policies, are endorsed. Family violence against Indigenous women requires further strategies that take into account the long-term impact of racism and colonialism.

In addition to these measures, others suggest a local community approach to domestic violence, which would require increased funding for outreach and advocacy services. As former Nardine worker Kedy Kristal reminds us, 'there's a huge number of women out there that are doing it alone or doing it just with family or friends'. Eighty per cent of women who experienced violence from a partner in the last twenty years sought no help from any services.[24] Others argue that there will never be enough money to meet the needs of those experiencing domestic violence. Therefore, according to social work academic Marilyn Palmer, we should be enriching communities to support and prevent domestic violence themselves.[25]

While there have been substantial changes in human service responses to domestic violence over the twentieth century, as former Western Australian Member of Parliament and Minister for Women's Interests Judyth Watson has asserted, 'there is no room for complacency'.[26] Maintaining a framework of understanding that places domestic violence within its wider social context of masculine advantage, as presented by feminists since the 1970s, is a critical aspect that social policy and program developers must bear in mind.

The final, optimistic words are left for two former residents of Nardine who both went on to work at the refuge. Their comments suggest that, for some at least, there has been change and it leaves space for further possibilities. Anna Spencer first came to Nardine in the mid-1970s:

I'm very grateful for the days that I was associated with Nardine. I often think that my life might have been considerably different had I not had that experience. For example, the two year old at the time is now twenty-four and it's really lovely to see women of her age group being so vastly different in terms of their expectations of life, their relationships, their values, the confidence that they have, the things that they reach for, all of those sorts of things. When I compare myself in that age group with seeing my daughter now, it's a joy to see all of what has happened in the past twenty years.[27]

Maggie Lawson came to Nardine around the same time as Spencer, and she, too, is also hopeful about changes that have occurred. She focuses on personal empowerment, indicating how the politicization of domestic violence has led to social change. Lawson describes women coming to refuges today, compared to when she arrived at Nardine, as 'braver, bolder, more confident. They know their rights, they know they don't have to put up with it, they know they are not to blame'.[28]

To some extent, the personal has been made political, but there is still the need for more than refuge.

# Notes

## Abbreviations used in Notes

| | |
|---|---|
| ABS | Australian Bureau of Statistics |
| AGPS | Australian Government Publishing Service |
| DCD | Department for Community Development |
| DCS | Department for Community Services |
| DCSH | Department of Community Services and Health |
| DCW | Department for Community Welfare |
| DPMC | Department of Prime Minister and Cabinet |
| DVCC | Domestic Violence Coordinating Committee |
| DVPU | Domestic Violence Prevention Unit |
| DVTF | Domestic Violence Task Force |
| FCS | Department for Family and Children's Services |
| FDVT | Family and Domestic Violence Taskforce |
| IWY | International Women's Year |
| NCVAW | National Committee on Violence Against Women |
| NSW | New South Wales |
| OSW | Office of the Status of Women |
| PADV | Partnerships Against Domestic Violence |
| PCC | Perth City Council |
| SAAP | Supported Accommodation Assistance Program |
| SCWA | Supreme Court of Western Australia |
| SROWA | State Records Office of Western Australia |
| UWA | University of Western Australia |
| WA | Western Australia/Western Australian |

| WAPD | *Western Australian Parliamentary Debates* |
| WCAG | Women's Centre Action Group |
| WCTU | Women's Christian Temperance Union |
| WEL | Women's Electoral Lobby |
| WESNET | Women's Emergency Services Network |
| WHCC | Women's Health and Community Centre |
| WPDO | Women's Policy Development Office |
| WPO | Women's Policy Office |
| WRG | Women's Refuge Group |

## Notes to Introduction: Making the personal political

1 Ann Curthoys, 'Doing it for themselves: The Women's Movement since 1970', in Kay Saunders & Raymond Evans (eds), *Gender Relations in Australia: Domination and Negotiation*, Sydney, Harcourt Brace, 1992, p. 425.

2 ABS, *Women's Safety Australia*, catalogue no. 4128.0, 1996, p. 50.

3 Fran Ellery, *Costs of Domestic Violence: New South Wales Domestic Violence Strategic Plan*, Sydney, NSW Women's Coordination Unit, 1991. See also Monika Henderson, *Impacts and Costs of Domestic Violence on the Australian Business/Corporate Sector*, Lord Mayor's Women's Advisory Committee, Brisbane, 2000; OSW, DPMC, *Working Together Against Violence: The First Three Years of Partnerships Against Domestic Violence*, Canberra, Commonwealth of Australia, 2001, pp. 14–15.

4 In 1987, the spelling was changed to Nardine Wimmin's Refuge. The former version is used in this book.

5 For a brief discussion of the language of naming domestic violence in Australia, see Lesley Laing, 'Progress, trends and challenges in Australian responses to domestic violence', *Issues Paper 1*, Sydney, Australian Domestic and Family Violence Clearinghouse, 2000, pp. 1–2. Elsewhere in Australia and internationally, other terms have been used—for example, 'family violence', which at times has included other forms of interpersonal violence such as child abuse.

6 PADV, *First Report of the Taskforce, 1998–1999*, Canberra, Commonwealth of Australia, 1999, p. 2.

7 DVPU, *Best Practice Model for the Provision of Programs for Victims of Domestic Violence in Western Australia*, Perth, WA Government, 1999, p. 5.

8 See, for example, Kerrie James, 'Truth or fiction: Men as victims of domestic violence?', in Jan Breckenridge & Lesley Laing (eds), *Challenging Silence: Innovative Responses to Sexual and Domestic Violence*, Sydney, Allen & Unwin,

1999, pp. 153–62; Sotirios Sarantakos, 'Husband abuse: Fact or fiction?', *Australian Journal of Social Issues*, vol. 34, no. 3, 1999, pp. 231–52; and see Dale Bagshaw & Donna Chung, *Women, Men and Violence*, University of South Australia, 2000, for an explanation of these differing points of view.

9  Laing, 'Progress, trends and challenges', p. 4.

10  Anna Ferrante, Frank Morgan, David Indermaur & Richard Harding, *Measuring the Extent of Domestic Violence*, Sydney, Hawkins Press, 1996, p. 29.

11  For a discussion of radical feminism, see, for example, Rosemarie Tong, *Feminist Thought: A More Comprehensive Introduction*, Sydney, Allen & Unwin, 1998; Hester Eisenstein, *Contemporary Feminist Thought*, Sydney, Allen & Unwin, 1984.

12  Patricia Grimshaw, Marilyn Lake, Ann McGrath & Marian Quartly, *Creating a Nation, 1788–1990*, Melbourne, McPhee Gribble, 1994, pp. 3–4.

13  ibid., p. 4.

### Notes to Chapter 1: From protection to empowerment: A background to feminist politics

1  Marilyn Lake, *Getting Equal: The History of Australian Feminism*, Sydney, Allen & Unwin, 1999, p. 4.

2  ibid., pp. 50–1.

3  ibid., p. 56.

4  Marilyn Lake, 'The inviolable woman: Feminist conceptions of citizenship in Australia, 1900–1945', in Jane Long, Jan Gothard & Helen Brash (eds), *Forging Identities: Bodies, Gender and Feminist History*, Perth, UWA Press, 1997, p. 242.

5  ibid., p. 231; Lake, *Getting Equal*, pp. 56–9.

6  Lake, *Getting Equal*, p. 71.

7  See Gail Reekie, 'With ready hands and new brooms: The women who campaigned for female suffrage in Western Australia, 1895–1899', *Hecate*, vol. 7, no. 1, pp. 24–35. See also Katie Spearritt, 'New dawns: First wave feminism, 1880–1914', in Kay Saunders & Raymond Evans (eds), *Gender Relations in Australia: Domination and Negotiation*, Sydney, Harcourt Brace, 1992, pp. 325–49, for a discussion with an emphasis on activities in Victoria and New South Wales.

8  I. McCorkindale, *Frances E. Willard Centenary Book* (3rd edn), Adelaide, WCTU, 1940, p. 31, cited in 'A Feminine Temperance: The Women's Christian Temperance Union of Western Australia, 1892–1900', 1975, p. 2, unpublished paper, held in Battye Library.

9  Lake, *Getting Equal*, pp. 53–5. See also Marilyn Lake, 'Mother, race and nation in a welfare state', in Patricia Crawford & Judy Skene (eds), *Women*

*and Citizenship: Suffrage Centenary*, vol. 19, *Studies in Western Australian History*, 1999, pp. 116–17.

10  *Dawn*, 12 February 1921, and *West Australian*, 12 February 1921, cited in Lake, *Getting Equal*, p. 54.

11  Peter Cowan, *A Unique Position: A Biography of Edith Dircksey Cowan, 1861–1932*, Nedlands, UWA Press, 1978.

12  ibid., pp. 44–5. Thanks to Alanna Clohesy for alerting me to this event.

13  *Daily News*, 21 July 1891, cited in ibid., pp. 90–1.

14  Cowan, *A Unique Position*, p. 91.

15  Dianne Davidson, *Women on the Warpath: Feminists of the First Wave*, Nedlands, UWA Press, 1997, p. 83.

16  ibid.

17  Bobbie Oliver, '"A truly great Australian woman": Jean Beadle's work among Western Australian women and children, 1901–1942', in Crawford & Skene (eds), *Women and Citizenship*, pp. 87–98. See also Lake, *Getting Equal*, pp. 55–7.

18  Claire Ozich, '"The great bond of motherhood": Maternal citizenship and Perth feminists in the 1920s', in Crawford & Skene (eds), *Women and Citizenship*, pp. 127–38.

19  Lake, *Getting Equal*, pp. 93–6.

20  ibid., p. 19. See Janet McCalman, *Sex and Suffering: Women's Health and a Women's Hospital*, Melbourne, Melbourne University Press, 1998, for a discussion of Australian women's reproductive ill health.

21  Salvation Army Graceville Women's Centre, *1990–91 Annual Report*, p. 1; Salvation Army Graceville Women's Centre, *Annual Report, 1985*, p. 6.

22  *West Australian*, 1 June 1961, p. 25.

23  Michelle White, 'Women's Refuges: A Focus for the Marginalisation of Single Parents in Australian Society', Hons thesis, Department of History, UWA, 1991. See also Heather McGregor & Andrew Hopkins, *Working for Change: The Movement against Domestic Violence*, Sydney, Allen & Unwin, 1991, p. 12.

24  Lake, *Getting Equal*, p. 173.

25  ibid., p. 4.

26  ibid., p. 174.

27  ibid., p. 173.

28  ibid., p. 176.

29  *Broadsheet*, vol. 5, no. 5, October 1977, pp. 6–7.

30  For a discussion of the peace activism of Joan Williams, Bernice Ranford, Elsie Gare and Margaret Davis, see Lekkie Hopkins, 'Fighting to be seen and heard: A tribute to four Western Australian peace activists', *Women's Studies International Forum*, vol. 22, no. 1, 1999, pp. 79–87.

31 Lake, *Getting Equal*, p. 207.
32 Gail Reekie, 'War, sexuality and feminism: Perth women's organisations, 1938–1945', *Historical Studies*, vol. 21, no. 85, 1985, pp. 576–91.

**Notes to Chapter 2: Establishing a feminist refuge: Nardine as a 1970s response to domestic violence**

1 Michele Kosky, describing the manner in which Nardine was set up; interviewed by Suellen Murray, 17 March 1998.
2 See Jocelynne Scutt, 'Inequality before the law: Gender, arbitration and wages', in Kay Saunders & Raymond Evans (eds), *Gender Relations in Australia: Domination and Negotiation*, Sydney, Harcourt Brace, 1992, pp. 266–86.
3 See Ann Curthoys, 'Doing it for themselves: The Women's Movement since 1970', in Saunders & Evans (eds), *Gender Relations in Australia*, pp. 436–7. For a history of the development of child-care services in Australia, see Deborah Brennan, *The Politics of Australian Child Care: Philanthropy to Feminism and Beyond*, Melbourne, Cambridge University Press, 1998.
4 For a brief discussion of the difficulties that Australian women faced in getting out of marriages prior to the 1970s, see Gisela Kaplan, *The Meagre Harvest: The Australian Women's Movement, 1950s–1990s*, Sydney, Allen & Unwin, 1996, pp. 188–9. See also Eversley Ruth, *Divorce: Window on the Gender War*, Perth, Evergreen, 1987, pp. 11–24.
5 Brennan, *The Politics of Australian Child Care*, p. 70.
6 Curthoys, 'Doing it for themselves', pp. 429–32; Marilyn Lake, *Getting Equal: The History of Australian Feminism*, Sydney, Allen & Unwin, 1999, pp. 220–2.
7 Lake, *Getting Equal*, pp. 222–3, 227–8. For a personal account of these early days of women's liberation in Adelaide and Sydney, see Anne Summers, *Ducks on the Pond: An Autobiography 1945–1976*, Melbourne, Viking, 1999.
8 Lake, *Getting Equal*, pp. 233–5.
9 *Liberation Information*, January 1973, p. 2; also cited in Lake, *Getting Equal*, p. 235.
10 Pat Giles, interviewed by Maureen Davies, *Sibyl*, no. 7, April 1976. See also Pat Giles, interviewed by Sally Speed, 10 August 1982, held in Battye Library, OH1105.
11 *Liberation Information*, March 1973; also cited in Lake, *Getting Equal*, p. 233.
12 *Liberation Information*, April–May 1973, p. 1.
13 Giles interview (1976). See also Wendy Fatin and Pat Giles, both interviewed by Sally Speed, 10 August 1982, held in Battye Library, OH1105; and *Broadsheet*, 'History of WEL Perth', special national conference issue, 1976, p. 2, for further discussion of the setting up of WEL in Perth.

14 *Sibyl*, vol. 1, no. 1, 1974, p. 13.

15 Heather McGregor & Andrew Hopkins, *Working for Change: The Movement against Domestic Violence*, Sydney, Allen & Unwin, 1991, p. 4.

16 Michele Kosky, interviewed by Pascale Gilham, May 1997; Michele Kosky, interviewed by Suellen Murray, 17 March 1998 (further comments attributed to Kosky are from the latter source). See also Australian National Advisory Committee, IWY, *Newsletter*, no. 1, December 1974, pp. 1–2.

17 *Broadsheet*, vol. 2, no. 2, June 1974, p. 3.

18 Kosky interview.

19 Erin Pizzey, *Scream Quietly or the Neighbours Will Hear*, Melbourne, Penguin, 1974.

20 Quoted in ibid., p. 19.

21 For media interest in Western Australia, see, for example, 'Women in terror', *Sunday Times*, 18 August 1974, p. 45.

22 Quoted in Summers, *Ducks on the Pond*, p. 319.

23 ibid., p. 316.

24 ibid., pp. 320–7. See also Mark Lyons, Julie Nyland & Sallie Saunders, 'Moving in from the fringe', in Felice Davidson Perlmutter (ed.), *Women and Social Change: Nonprofit and Social Policy*, Washington, NASW Press, 1994.

25 McGregor & Hopkins, *Working for Change*, p. 11.

26 *History of WEL Inc., 1973–1984*, Perth, c. 1985, p. 118; *Broadsheet*, vol. 2, no. 2, June 1974, p. 10.

27 *Broadsheet*, vol. 2, no. 2, June 1974, p. 3.

28 WCAG, 'Submission for financial assistance for Nardine Women's Refuge', 1974, Nardine archives; Women's Liberation of Western Australia, *Newsletter*, June 1974, p. 1; *Broadsheet*, vol. 2, no. 2, June 1974, p. 10.

29 WCAG, 'Submission for financial assistance'.

30 Ludo McFerren, 'Interpretation of a frontline state: Australian women's refuges and the state', in Sophie Watson (ed.), *Playing the State: Australian Feminist Interventions*, Sydney, Allen & Unwin, 1990, p. 193.

31 ibid.; see also Ludo McFerran, *Beyond the Image: Women's Emergency Services Programme Evaluation*, Perth, WA Government, 1987, p. 29.

32 Kosky interview.

33 *West Australian*, 17 July 1974, p. 42.

34 ibid.

35 Kosky interview.

36 'Basic facts concerning Nardine', May 1975, private collection.

37 *Broadsheet*, vol. 2, no. 5, August 1974, p. 8.

38 *Broadsheet*, vol. 2, no. 8, November 1974, p. 8.

39 ibid.

40 Nardine archives, 1975, Lespar Library.

41 WCAG, *News Sheet*, no. 3, 19 January 1975, Nardine archives.

42 Royal Commission on Human Relationships, *Final Report*, vol. 4, part V, *The Family*, Canberra, AGPS, 1977, p. 147.

43 *WCAG Newsletter*, no. 8, September–October 1975.

44 Deborah Dearnley, interviewed by Suellen Murray, 15 May 1998 (further comments attributed to Dearnley are from this source).

45 'Nardine Women's Refuge procedures', March 1976, WHCC archives, Lespar Library.

46 *Broadsheet*, vol. 3, no. 10, March 1976, p. 10; ephemera, 1976, WHCC archives, Lespar Library.

47 Anna Spencer (pseudonym), interviewed by Suellen Murray, 17 March 1998 (further comments attributed to Spencer are from this source). For legal reasons, former residents are not identified.

48 Women's Liberation of Western Australia, *Newsletter*, June 1974, p. 2.

49 'Establishing the Nardine Collective', c. 1975, WHCC archives, Lespar Library.

50 See, for example, *Women's Refuge Group Newsletter*, vol. 5, no. 1, 2000.

51 Sue Allen, interviewed by Suellen Murray, 5 June 1998 (further comments attributed to Allen are from this source).

52 Michelle Scott, interviewed by Suellen Murray, 7 December 1999.

53 McFerran, *Beyond the Image*, p. 32.

54 ibid., p. 1.

55 Diana Warnock, interviewed by Suellen Murray, 5 October 1999.

56 *West Australian*, 6 August 1977, p. 21; *WAPD*, 3 August 1977, pp. 197–8.

57 Allen interview.

58 'One more time with feeling', *Around the Cauldron: A Perth Wimin's Liberation Magazine*, Perth, c. 1980, p. 17.

59 Dianne Otto & Eileen Haley, 'Helter shelter: A history of the Adelaide women's shelter', *Refractory Girl*, Winter, 1975, p. 15.

60 *Liberation Information*, July 1974.

61 Sally Speed, 'Women's Centre Action Group, Women's Health and Community Centre: A Resume of the History So Far', March 1975, private collection.

62 *Liberation Information*, July 1974.

63 'Nardine's finances', Nardine archives; WHCC archives, Lespar Library.

64 *Broadsheet*, vol. 3, no. 1, May 1975, p. 9; Gillian Draffin, 'Politics of establishing women's health centres', in DPMC, *Women and Politics Conference, 1975*, Canberra, AGPS, 1975, pp. 46–50, 52–3.

65 Marian Sawer, *Sisters in Suits: Women and Public Policy in Australia*, Sydney, Allen & Unwin, 1990, pp. 12–13.

66 For discussions of the effects of changing political climates on Nardine during these early years, see McFerran, *Beyond the Image*, pp. 29–44; and McFerren, 'Interpretation of a frontline state', pp. 191–205. This is discussed further in chapter 3.

67 Maggie Lawson (pseudonym), interviewed by Suellen Murray, 3 March 1998. For further discussion of the low wages paid to refuge workers, see McFerren, 'Interpretation of a frontline state', p. 199.

68 For a discussion of radical feminism, see, for example, Rosemarie Tong, *Feminist Thought: A More Comprehensive Introduction*, Sydney, Allen & Unwin, 1998.

69 For a discussion of the term 'patriarchy' as understood during the 1970s, see Ann Curthoys, 'The Women's Movement and social justice', in Dorothy Broom (ed.), *Unfinished Business: Social Justice for Women in Australia*, Sydney, Allen & Unwin, 1984, pp. 160–1.

70 Michaela Kronemann, 'Modern feminist theory', in Norma Grieve & Patricia Grimshaw (eds), *Australian Women: Feminist Perspectives*, Melbourne, Oxford University Press, 1981, p. 216.

71 'A personal view of a feminist collective', *Around the Cauldron: A Perth Wimin's Liberation Magazine*, Perth, c. 1980, p. 18.

72 Heather Goodall & Jackie Huggins, 'Aboriginal women are everywhere: Contemporary struggles', in Saunders & Evans (eds), *Gender Relations in Australia*, p. 416.

73 Dearnley interview.

74 McFerran, *Beyond the Image*, p. 12.

75 *Broadsheet*, vol. 4, no. 3, August 1976, pp. 6–7. See also *Broadsheet*, vol. 4, no. 1, June 1976, p. 13.

### Notes to Chapter 3: Feminism in action: Philosophy and practice at Nardine

1 Sue Allen discussing what empowerment meant to her; interviewed by Suellen Murray, 5 June 1998 (further comments attributed to Allen are from this source).

2 WRG, *Submission to the Domestic Violence Task Force*, August 1985, p. 3.

3 ibid., p. 4.

4 Merrill Findlay, 'Women's refuges', *Girl About Town*, no. 5, August 1981, p. 85.

5 Maggie Lawson (pseudonym), interviewed by Suellen Murray, 3 March 1998 (further comments attributed to Lawson are from this source).

6 Anna Spencer (pseudonym), interviewed by Suellen Murray, 17 March 1998 (further comments attributed to Spencer are from this source).

7 Deborah Dearnley, interviewed by Suellen Murray, 15 May 1998 (further comments attributed to Dearnley are from this source).

8 Libby Best, interviewed by Suellen Murray, 26 January 1998.

9 Glenda Blake, interviewed by Suellen Murray, 29 July 1998.

10 Dearnley interview.

11 Blake interview (further comments attributed to Blake are from this source).

12 Kedy Kristal, interviewed by Suellen Murray, 28 June 2000 (further comments attributed to Kristal are from this source).

13 Daphne Smith, interviewed by Suellen Murray, 26 May 1998 (further comments attributed to Smith are from this source).

14 Best interview (further comments attributed to Best are from this source).

15 *Grapevine*, no. 67, August 1986, p. 8.

16 Diana Warnock, interviewed by Suellen Murray, 5 October 1999 (further comments attributed to Warnock are from this source).

17 *WCAG Newsletter*, no. 8, September–October 1975.

18 Best interview.

19 See, for example, DCS, *Working with Women and Children in Refuges: A Training Package for Refuge Workers on Domestic Violence*, Perth, DCS/DCSH, 1990, pp. 21–2; Ian Macdonald, 'The cyclic pattern of abusive relationships', Queensland Marriage Council, 1987, for discussion of the cycle of violence; and Ellen Rence, *In Our Best Interest: A Process for Personal and Social Change*, 1987, cited in DCS, *Spouse Abuse: Guidelines to Practice*, Perth, DCS, 1990, on the 'Power and Control Wheel' developed by the Domestic Abuse Intervention Project, Duluth, Minnesota, United States.

20 Cath Munro, interviewed by Suellen Murray, 6 June 1998 (further comments attributed to Munro are from this source).

21 Michele Kosky, interviewed by Suellen Murray, 17 March 1998; Susie Strong, interviewed by Suellen Murray, 5 October 1999. (Further comments attributed to Kosky and Strong are from these sources.)

22 Untitled submission, c. 1976, Nardine archives.

23 *WCAG News Sheet*, no. 5, 15 May 1975.

24 For reiteration of these comments, see submission, 'Details of further staff and facilities required at Nardine Women's Refuge, 1976', Nardine archives.

25 Jill Bowen, 'What makes a wife run away?', *Australian Women's Weekly*, 21 January 1976, pp. 28–9.

26 Dearnley interview.

27 Best interview.

28 For discussion of the effects of domestic violence on children and young people, see, for example, Maryon Allbrook, *Break the Cycle: The Extent and Effects on Young People of Witnessing Domestic Violence*, Perth, Youth Affairs Council of Western Australia, 1992; Anne Blanchard, *Caring for Child Victims of Domestic Violence*, Perth, Nardina Press, 1999; Lesley Laing, 'Children, young people and domestic violence', *Issues Paper 2*, Sydney, Australian Domestic and Family Violence Clearinghouse, 2000.

29 Ludo McFerran, *Beyond the Image: Women's Emergency Services Programme Evaluation*, WA Government, 1987, pp. 112–26. See also DVTF, *Break the Silence*, Perth, WA Government, 1986, pp. 136–7; Colleen Chesterman,

*Homes Away from Home: Supported Accommodation Assistance Program Review*, Canberra, AGPS, 1988, pp. 64–5.

30 Findlay, 'Women's refuges', p. 86.

31 'Basic facts concerning Nardine', May 1975, private collection.

32 Findlay, 'Women's refuges', p. 86.

33 *Grapevine*, no. 67, August 1986, p. 8.

34 Munro interview.

35 Linda Digby, interviewed by Suellen Murray, 6 August 1998 (further comments attributed to Digby are from this source).

36 ibid.

37 Wendy Weeks, *Women Working Together: Lessons from Feminist Women's Services*, Melbourne, Longman Cheshire, 1994, pp. 134–41, 307, 315–16.

38 For discussion of the tensions between government and feminist collectives, see Rose-Lyn Melville, 'The external organisational environment and organisational survival and change', *Third Sector Review*, vol. 1, 1995, pp. 65–77.

39 While Nicholls made the decision to end the collective basis on which Nardine worked, he did not oversee the implementation of this measure. In 1996, he ceased to be the Minister for Family and Children's Services. For commentary, see, for example, *WAPD*, 11 April 1995, pp. 1115–37; 11 May 1995, pp. 2814–24; 28 June 1995, pp. 6139–51; 7 December 1995, pp. 12768–73.

40 Digby interview.

41 *Grapevine*, no. 67, August 1986, p. 8.

42 Joan Groves, interviewed by Suellen Murray, 9 March 1998.

43 Blake interview.

44 Groves interview.

45 Allen interview. The difficulties of the informal processes of power and other 'pitfalls' of collectives are elaborated on in Weeks, *Women Working Together*, pp. 138–9.

46 Best interview.

47 McFerran, *Beyond the Image*, p. 19. A women's refuge training program was developed and first run in 1990.

48 Best interview.

49 Gisela Kaplan, *The Meagre Harvest: The Australian Women's Movement, 1950s–1990s*, Sydney, Allen & Unwin, 1996, p. 58.

50 Best interview.

51 Tim Atkinson, 'Sisters are doing it for themselves', *West Australian*, 26 July 1988, p. 11.

52 Kerreen Reiger, '"Sort of part of the women's movement, but different": Mothers' organisations and Australian feminism', *Women's Studies International Forum*, vol. 22, no. 6, p. 592.

53 Groves interview.
54 See Adrienne Rich, 'Compulsory heterosexuality and lesbian existence', *Signs*, vol. 5, no. 4, 1980, pp. 631–60. See also Kaplan, *The Meagre Harvest*, ch. 4, and especially pp. 98–103, for further discussion of lesbians, sexuality and the women's movement.

**Notes to Chapter 4: Making sense of domestic violence: History, discourse and lived experience**

1 Glenda Blake, commenting on coming to work at Nardine in the early 1980s; interviewed by Suellen Murray, 29 July 1998 (further comments attributed to Blake are from this source).
2 Old English saying, cited in Merrill Findlay, 'Women's refuges', *Girl About Town*, no. 5, August 1981, p. 84.
3 DVTF, *Break the Silence*, Perth, WA Government, 1986, p. 40; Betsy Wearing, *Gender: The Pain and Pleasure of Difference*, Melbourne, Longman, 1996, pp. 196–7. The *Married Women's Property Act 1892* was a significant milestone that allowed for women to own property in their own right, enter into contracts, etc.
4 *Blackstones Commentaries*, 1763, cited in DVTF, *Break the Silence*, p. 40. See also Kim Rooney, 'Dealing with domestic violence in WA', *Legal Service Bulletin*, vol. 8, no. 5, 1983, p. 205.
5 See, for example, W. Cooper, *Flagellation and the Flagellants: A History of the Rod in all Countries*, London, Reeves, 1860, p. 388, cited in DVTF, *Break the Silence*, pp. 40–1.
6 Statutes of WA, 27 Vic., 19, 1863.
7 See Margaret Anderson, '"Helpmeet for man": Women in mid-nineteenth century Western Australia', in Patricia Crawford (ed.), *Exploring Women's Past*, Melbourne, Sisters Publishing, 1983, p. 118; Marian Aveling, *Westralian Voices*, Perth, UWA Press, 1979, pp. 323–7. For discussion in the Western Australian Parliament, see, for example, *WAPD*, 16 November 1911, pp. 300–3; 21 November 1911, pp. 316–22; 28 November 1911, pp. 466–73; 5 December 1911, pp. 593–608.
8 Statutes of WA, 43 Vic., 9, 1879.
9 Margaret Grellier, 'The family: Some aspects of its demography and ideology in mid-nineteenth century Western Australia', in Tom Stannage (ed.), *A New History of Western Australia*, Perth, UWA Press, 1981, p. 502; Anderson, '"Helpmeet for man"', pp. 118–19.
10 Anderson, '"Helpmeet for man"', pp. 119–20.
11 MSS, Record Books, *Divorce and Matrimonial Causes Act*, 1863–1900, SCWA, entry for 1886, cited in Anderson, '"Helpmeet for man"', p. 122. See also Aveling, *Westralian Voices*, pp. 323–7.

12 See, for example, Judith Allen, 'The invention of the pathological family: A historical study of family violence in New South Wales', in Carol O'Donnell & Jan Craney (eds), *Family Violence in Australia*, Melbourne, Longman Cheshire, 1982, pp. 1–27; Raymond Evans, 'A gun in the oven: Masculinism and gendered violence', in Kay Saunders & Raymond Evans (eds), *Gender Relations in Australia: Domination and Negotiation*, Sydney, Harcourt Brace, 1992, pp. 197–218; Marilyn Lake, 'The politics of respectability: Identifying the masculinist context', *Historical Studies*, vol. 22, 1986, pp. 123–4; Kay Saunders, 'The study of domestic violence in colonial Queensland: Sources and problems', *Historical Studies*, vol. 21, 1984.

13 Grellier, 'The family', pp. 501–4.

14 Statutes of WA, 60 Vic., 10, 1896.

15 *WAPD*, 5 August 1896, p. 262.

16 ibid., p. 263.

17 Statutes of WA, 60 Vic., 10, 1896.

18 Cons 3404, 1/1905, *Divorce and Matrimonial Causes Act*, SCWA, held at SROWA.

19 Cons 3404, 46/1920, *Divorce and Matrimonial Causes Act*, SCWA, held at SROWA.

20 See, for example, Cons 3404, 119/1919, 53/1920, *Divorce and Matrimonial Causes Act*, SCWA, held at SROWA.

21 *WAPD*, 29 August 1922, p. 451.

22 ibid. This is not actually correct. As noted by the Hon. T. Walker, Member for Kanowna, the existing legislation already provided for a wife to seek judicial separation without her husband being convicted of assault.

23 *WAPD*, 29 August 1922, p. 452.

24 ibid.

25 *Matrimonial Causes Act 1959*, 413 of 1961, held at SCWA.

26 *WAPD*, 27 October 1960, p. 2208. See also comments in a similar vein by the Hon. R. F. Hutchinson, *WAPD*, 15 November 1960, p. 2716.

27 *Matrimonial Causes Act 1959*, 413 of 1961, held at SCWA.

28 *Matrimonial Causes Act 1959*, 183 of 1962, held at SCWA.

29 *Matrimonial Causes Act 1959*, 365 of 1944, held at SCWA.

30 *Matrimonial Causes Act 1959*, 423 of 1961, held at SCWA.

31 *Matrimonial Causes Act 1959*, 496 of 1961, held at SCWA.

32 *Matrimonial Causes Act 1959*, 160 of 1944, held at SCWA.

33 Acc. 1042, AN 47/2, item 5128/1929, held at SROWA.

34 Elizabeth Evatt, paper presented as the Sir Robert Garran Memorial Oration, Adelaide, 15 November 1978, cited in Donald E. Stewart & Margaret Harrison, *Divorce in Australia*, Melbourne, Institute of Family Studies, 1982, p. 1.

35 Ailsa Burns, *Breaking Up: Separation and Divorce in Australia*, Melbourne, Nelson, 1980, pp. ix, 119.

36 ibid., pp. 46–8.

37 Michele Kosky, interviewed by Suellen Murray, 17 March 1998.

38 Royal Commission on Human Relationships, *Final Report*, vol. 4, part V, *The Family*, Canberra, AGPS, 1977, p. 133.

39 ibid.

40 ibid., pp. 137–8.

41 Evans, 'A gun in the oven', p. 201.

42 Jerzey Krupinski & Valerie Yule, 'Family conflict and family disruption', in Jerzey Krupinski & Alan Stoller (eds), *The Family in Australia*, Sydney, Pergamon, 1974, cited in Wearing, *Gender*, pp. 121–2.

43 DCW, *Annual Report 1982/83*, Perth, WA Government, 1983, pp. 43–4. Other categories included parent–child discord, child abuse and material needs.

44 DCW, *Annual Report 1983/84*, Perth, WA Government, 1984, pp. 50–1.

45 Judith Healy, 'Averting the public gaze: Social work's response to battered wives', *Australian Social Work*, vol. 37, no. 2, 1984, p. 6.

46 DCW, *Annual Report 1977*, Perth, WA Government, 1978, p. 35.

47 Eversley Ruth, *Divorce: Window on the Gender War*, Perth, Evergreen, 1987, pp. 93–4.

48 *Matrimonial Causes Act 1959*, 1065 of 1974, held at SCWA.

49 *Matrimonial Causes Act 1959*, 988 of 1974, held at SCWA.

50 *Matrimonial Causes Act 1959*, 780 of 1974, held at SCWA. See also 887 of 1974.

51 Maggie Lawson (pseudonym), interviewed by Suellen Murray, 3 March 1998.

52 Daphne Smith, interviewed by Suellen Murray, 26 May 1998 (further comments attributed to Smith are from this source).

53 Diana Warnock, interviewed by Suellen Murray, 5 October 1999.

54 Deborah Dearnley, interviewed by Suellen Murray, 15 May 1998.

55 Anna Spencer (pseudonym), interviewed by Suellen Murray, 17 March 1998.

56 Kay Hallahan, interviewed by Suellen Murray, 7 December 1999.

57 See Jocelynne Scutt, *Even in the Best of Homes: Violence in the Family*, Melbourne, Penguin, 1983, pp. 105–31.

58 For an example of a Perth woman's experience of a 'reign of terror', see *Sibyl*, no. 4, 1975, pp. 8–9.

59 DCS, *Spouse Abuse: Guidelines to Practice*, Perth, DCS, 1990, p. 19.

60 R. V. Almeida & T. Durkin, 'The cultural context: Therapy for couples with domestic violence', *Journal of Marital and Family Therapy*, vol. 25, 1999, p. 313, cited in Lesley Laing, 'Progress, trends and challenges in Australian

responses to domestic violence', *Issues Paper 1*, Sydney, Australian Domestic and Family Violence Clearinghouse, 2000, p. 1.

61 *Agenda*, vol. 3, no. 2, June 2000, p. 1.

62 *Agenda*, vol. 1, no. 1, September 1998, p. 1.

63 For discussion of criminal justice interventions, see Robyn Holder, 'Domestic and family violence: Criminal justice interventions', *Issues Paper 3*, Sydney, Australian Domestic and Family Violence Clearinghouse, 2001. See also Jennifer Gardiner, *Literature Review on Models of Coordination and Integration of Service Delivery*, Perth, DVPU, 2000.

64 Seymane's case, 1604, cited in Scutt, *Even in the Best of Homes*.

65 Marilyn Lake, *Getting Equal: The History of Australian Feminism*, Sydney, Allen & Unwin, 1999, p. 204.

66 Wearing, *Gender*, pp. 117–18.

67 ibid., p. 120.

68 *Sunday Times*, 7 September 1980, cited in *WAPD*, 5 November 1980, p. 3028.

69 *WAPD*, 5 November 1980, p. 3028.

70 Office of the Family, *Annual Report 1989/1990*, Perth, WA Government, 1990, p. 3.

71 DCS, *Domestic Violence Policy*, Perth, WA Government, c. 1990.

72 Wearing, *Gender*, p. 124.

73 ibid., p. 125.

74 ibid., p. 95.

75 ibid., p. 85.

76 ibid.

77 *Women's Liberation of Western Australia Newsletter*, June 1974, p. 2.

78 Blake interview.

79 Lake, *Getting Equal*, p. 243.

80 Dianne Otto & Eileen Haley, 'Helter shelter: A history of the Adelaide women's shelter', *Refractory Girl*, Winter, 1975, p. 15.

**Notes to Chapter 5: Breaking the silence: Responses to domestic violence in the 1980s**

1 Ludo McFerrin, 'Domestic violence—stories, scandals and serious analysis', *Refracting Voices: Refractory Girl*, 44/45, 1993, p. 153.

2 Kay Hallahan, interviewed by Suellen Murray, 7 December 1999.

3 Michelle Scott, interviewed by Suellen Murray, 7 December 1999 (further comments attributed to Scott are from this source).

4 Hallahan interview.

5 Daphne Smith, interviewed by Suellen Murray, 26 May 1998 (further comments attributed to Smith are from this source).

6 Ludo McFerran, *Beyond the Image: Women's Emergency Services Programme Evaluation*, Perth, WA Government, 1987, p. 17.

7 Glenda Blake, interviewed by Suellen Murray, 29 July 1998 (further comments attributed to Blake are from this source).

8 WRG, 'Submission to Domestic Violence Task Force', August 1985.

9 Cath Munro, interviewed by Suellen Murray, 6 June 1998 (further comments attributed to Munro are from this source).

10 Deborah Dearnley, interviewed by Suellen Murray, 15 May 1998 (further comments attributed to Dearnley are from this source).

11 See McFerran, *Beyond the Image*, pp. 34–6, for a discussion of data collection and women's refuges.

12 Sue Allen, interviewed by Suellen Murray, 5 June 1998 (further comments attributed to Allen are from this source).

13 D. J. Wordsworth, MLC, representing the Minister for Health, in answer to a question put by Robert Hetherington, MLC, *WAPD*, 15 September 1981, p. 3595.

14 See, for example, Smith interview.

15 McFerran, *Beyond the Image*, p. 12.

16 Kedy Kristal, interviewed by Suellen Murray, 28 June 2000.

17 *WAPD*, 5 November 1980, p. 3028.

18 *WAPD*, 10 November 1981, p. 5400.

19 ibid.

20 *WAPD*, 23 September 1981, p. 3879.

21 DVTF, *Break the Silence*, Perth, WA Government, p. 127.

22 R. G. Pike, MLC, *WAPD*, 11 August 1982, pp. 2200–1.

23 *WAPD*, 27 July 1983, p. 335.

24 DCW, *Annual Report, 1984*, pp. 49–50. See also *WAPD*, 30 November 1983, p. 5598. The DVTF also noted the invisibility of domestic violence among the work of the Crisis Care Unit; see DVTF, *Break the Silence*, p. 128.

25 *WAPD*, 10 November 1981, p. 5376.

26 ibid., p. 5379.

27 ibid., pp. 5375–7.

28 ibid., pp. 5376, 5379, 5399.

29 Lyla Elliott, interviewed by Suellen Murray, 2 March 2001.

30 *WAPD*, 18 March 1982, p. 8; 22 December 1982, p. 5490; 27 July 1983, p. 335; 6 March 1985, p. 579. See also Kim Rooney, 'Dealing with domestic violence in WA', *Legal Service Bulletin*, vol. 8, no. 5, 1983, p. 205; DVTF, *Break the Silence*, ch. 6.

31 *WAPD*, 22 December 1982, p. 5940.

32 Women's Coordination Unit, *Report of the New South Wales Domestic Violence Committee*, Sydney, NSW Government, 1981; South Australian Domestic Violence Council, *Report and Recommendations on Law Reform*, Adelaide, Women's Advisory Unit, Department of Premier and Cabinet, 1981; Women's Information Switchboard, *Domestic Violence Phone-in Report*, Adelaide, Women's Advisory Unit, Department of Premier and Cabinet,

1981; DCD, *Domestic Violence: A Review of Current Services and a Strategy for the Future*, Darwin, Northern Territory Government, 1983.

33 'Door opens on violence', *West Australian*, 19 April 1985, p. 25.

34 DVTF, *Break the Silence*, p. viii.

35 Lois Gatley, interviewed by Suellen Murray, 17, 29 February 2000 (further comments attributed to Gatley are from this source).

36 Elliott interview (further comments attributed to Elliott are from this source, unless otherwise referenced).

37 DVTF, *Break the Silence*, p. 276.

38 ibid., p. 141.

39 ibid., p. iv.

40 *WAPD*, 30 June 1987, pp. 3246–7; 17 September 1987, pp. 3914–15.

41 *WAPD*, 31 May 1988, p. 739.

42 'A history of the Department for Community Welfare', *DCW 1978/9 Annual Report*, p. 18. Acknowledgment to Pat Giles for this insight.

43 DVTF, *Break the Silence*, p. 207.

44 Judyth Watson, interviewed by Suellen Murray, 9 December 1999.

45 DCS, *Spouse Abuse: Guidelines to Practice*, Perth, DCS, 1990.

46 DCS, *Directions for Community Welfare Services*, Perth, WA Government, 1987, pp. 7, 8, 10.

47 ibid., p. 11.

48 DVTF, *Break the Silence*, p. 149. See also WRG, 'Submission to the Domestic Violence Task Force', pp. 18–19.

49 *WAPD*, 28 November 1986, p. 5241.

50 McFerran, *Beyond the Image*, p. 209.

51 DCS, *Financial Assistance Branch Manual*, cited in DCS, *Spouse Abuse*, p. 36.

52 DVCC, *Report to the Community*, Perth, WA Government, 1990, p. 16.

53 McFerran, *Beyond the Image*, pp. 33–4.

54 *WAPD*, 5 April 1979, p. 298.

55 'Nardine Women's Refuge submission to the Commissioner of Public Health', 1981, Nardine archives.

56 *WAPD*, 25 March 1981, p. 127.

57 *WAPD*, 5 April 1979, pp. 297–8.

58 McFerran, *Beyond the Image*, p. 38; Ludo McFerren, 'Interpretation of a frontline state: Australian women's refuges and the state', in Sophie Watson (ed.), *Playing the State: Australian Feminist Interventions*, Sydney, Allen & Unwin, 1990, pp. 198–9; see also *WAPD*, 15 September 1981, pp. 3594–7.

59 *WAPD*, 10 November 1981, p. 5384.

60 McFerran, *Beyond the Image*, pp. 38–40.

61 ibid., p. 32.

62 'Nardine Women's Refuge submission', 1981.

63  See McFerran, *Beyond the Image*, p. 6, and DVTF, *Break the Silence*, pp. 210–11, for discussions of the poor image of women's refuges in the 1970s and 1980s. McFerran's title of the review of refuges attempts to encourage others to look 'beyond the image'.

64  McFerran, *Beyond the Image*, pp. 41–2; McFerren, 'Interpretation of a frontline state', pp. 200–1; *WAPD*, 27 July 1983, p. 335; on this latter point, see, for example, *Grapevine*, no. 67, August 1986, p. 8.

65  See, for example, Gatley interview.

66  McFerran, *Beyond the Image*, pp. 193–201.

67  Colleen Chesterman, *Homes Away from Home: Supported Accommodation Assistance Program Review*, Canberra, AGPS, 1988, p. 61.

68  ibid., pp. 57–60.

69  DVCC, *Report to the Community*, p. 4.

70  Pat Giles, interviewed by Suellen Murray, 6 April 2000.

71  DPMC, OSW, *Setting the Agenda: Report of the Consultations on the National Agenda for Women*, Canberra, AGPS, 1987, p. 1.

72  DPMC, OSW, *A Say, a Choice, a Fair Go: The Government's National Agenda for Women*, 1988, Canberra, AGPS, 1988, pp. 37–9.

73  ibid., p. 67.

74  DVCC, *Report to the Community*, p. 19.

75  Based on research conducted by the Commonwealth Government, 1987–88, and cited in Office of the Family, 'What Australians believe about domestic violence', *Domestic Violence Information Kit*, Perth, WA Government, 1990. See also DVCC, *Report to the Community*, p. 18.

76  Heather McGregor & Andrew Hopkins, *Working for Change: The Movement against Domestic Violence*, Sydney, Allen & Unwin, 1991, p. xix.

77  DVCC, *Report to the Community*, pp. 19–20.

78  ibid., p. 22.

79  Petition and protest letter to the Town Clerk, Perth City Council, 6 September 1985, Nardine archives.

80  Quoted in Katie Hansen, 'Protest at women's refuge proposal', *Southern Gazette*, 17 September 1985.

81  Quoted in Katie Hansen, 'Refuge: Readers respond', *Southern Gazette*, 24 September 1985.

82  Minutes of PCC meeting, October 1985.

83  Norm Aisbett, 'PCC wilts and bans a women's refuge', *Daily News*, July 1988; Report to PCC from City Planner, 27 April 1988, Nardine archives.

84  Letter from R. F. Dawson, PCC Town Clerk, 1 August 1988, Nardine archives.

85  Letter from the Minister for Planning, Pam Beggs, 10 April 1989, Nardine archives.

86  Anonymous letter to 'fellow resident', June 1989, Nardine archives.

87  Shaun Menegola, 'Plea to find base for refuge', *West Australian*, June 1989.
88  Letter from R. F. Dawson, Town Clerk, PCC, 28 June 1989, Nardine archives.
89  Letter from the Minister for Planning, Pam Beggs, 29 June 1989, Nardine archives.
90  DCS, *1990 Annual Report*, p. 5.

**Notes to Chapter 6: A police station, a post office and a women's refuge: Responses to domestic violence in the 1990s**

1  WPDO, *Final Report 1998/1999*, Perth, WA Government, 1999, p. 2.
2  Pat Giles, interviewed by Suellen Murray, 6 April 2000.
3  NCVAW, *National Strategy on Violence Against Women*, Canberra, Commonwealth of Australia, 1992, p. vii.
4  ibid., pp. 4, 5.
5  ibid., pp. 19–22.
6  OSW, DPMC, *Community Attitudes to Violence Against Women*, Canberra, AGPS, 1995.
7  OSW, DPMC, *Violence at Home: The Big Secret*, Canberra, AGPS, 1996.
8  *Declaration on the Elimination of Violence Against Women*, Resolution A/RES/48/104, adopted 20 December 1993, United Nations Department of Public Information, New York, 1997.
9  PADV, *First Report of the Taskforce, 1998–1999*, Canberra, Commonwealth of Australia, 1999, p. 2.
10  ibid., p. 1.
11  ibid.
12  Lee FitzRoy, 'Just outcomes for women? State responses to violence against women', in Linda Hancock (ed.), *Women, Public Policy and the State*, Melbourne, Macmillan, 1999; Wendy Weeks, 'Towards the prevention of violence and the creation of safe and supportive gender relations', in Wendy Weeks & Marjorie Quinn (eds), *Issues Facing Australian Families: Human Services Respond*, 3rd edn, Sydney, Longman, 2000; Wendy Weeks & Kate Gilmore, 'How violence against women became an issue on the national policy agenda', in Tony Dalton, Mary Draper, Wendy Weeks & John Wiseman (eds), *Making Social Policy in Australia: An Introduction*, Sydney, Allen & Unwin, 1996.
13  <http://www.osw.dpmc.gov.au>; <http://www.osw.dpmc.gov.au/3rd_combat_sexual_assault.cfm>
14  OSW, DPMC, *Women 2001*, Canberra, Commonwealth of Australia, 2001, p. 14; OSW, DPMC, *Working Together Against Violence: The First Three Years of Partnerships Against Domestic Violence*, Canberra, Commonwealth of Australia, 2001, p. 7.
15  WA Government, *Taking Action: Domestic Violence Programs and Policies*, Perth, WA Government, 1992, p. 3.

16 ibid., pp. 2–3.

17 ibid., p. 6.

18 ibid.

19 ibid., p. 12.

20 DCD, *Abuse in Families*, Perth, WA Government, 1994, p. 10.

21 ibid.

22 ibid., p. 6.

23 FCS, *Annual Report, 1996/97*, Perth, WA Government, 1997, pp. 21–2.

24 FCS, *Domestic Violence Policy*, WA Government, 2000, p. 1.

25 FDVT, *'It's Not Just a Domestic': An Action Plan on Family and Domestic Violence*, Perth, WA Government, 1995, p. i.

26 Carole Kagi, interviewed by Suellen Murray, 27 June 2000 (further comments attributed to Kagi are from this source).

27 WPDO, *A Portrait of Progress: Women in Western Australia, 1899–1999*, Perth, WA Government, 1999, p. 71; WPDO, *Best Practice Model for the Provision of Programs for Victims of Domestic Violence in Western Australia*, Perth, WA Government, 1999, p. 2.

28 Lois Gatley, interviewed by Suellen Murray, 17, 26 February 2000 (further comments attributed to Gatley are from this source).

29 DVPU, *Best Practice*, p. 1.

30 Gatley interview.

31 <http://www.mediastatements.wa.gov.au/media/media.nsf>

32 See Lee Tan, *Family Violence Data Collection: Review of Practices in the Pilbara and Kimberley Regions of WA*, South Hedland, Hedland College Social Research Centre, 1996; Helen Cheney, Kate Mackey & Margaret Robinson, *Restricted Access: Meeting the Legal Needs of North West Women*, South Hedland, Hedland College Social Research Centre, 1998.

33 See, for example, in relation to sexual assault services, Mailin Suchting, 'The case of the too hard basket: Investigating the connections between "ethnicity", "culture" and "access" to sexual assault services', in Jan Breckenridge & Lesley Laing (eds), *Challenging Silence: Innovative Responses to Sexual and Domestic Violence*, Sydney, Allen & Unwin, 1999, pp. 82–4.

34 Crime Research Centre, 'Estimating the Incidence and Prevalence of Domestic Violence in Western Australia', Perth, UWA, 1995, cited in FDVT, *'It's Not Just a Domestic'*, p. 9.

35 Pauline Bagdonavicius, FCS, correspondence, 17 July 2000; WPDO, *Building on Success: Government Two Year Plan for Women, 1999–2001*, vol. 2, Perth, WA Government, 1999, p. 11; OSW, *Women 2001*, p. 31.

36 DVPU, Aboriginal Family Violence Strategy, Draft 4, May 2000, p. 11.

37 SAAP, *State Advisory Committee Newsletter*, August 1999, insert; Bagdonavicius, correspondence.

38 FCS, *Annual Report 2000/2001*, Perth, WA Government, 2001, p. 42.

39 SAAP, *State Advisory Committee Newsletter*.

40 Kedy Kristal, interviewed by Suellen Murray, 28 June 2000 (further comments attributed to Kristal are from this source, unless otherwise referenced).

41 Bagdonavicius, correspondence.

42 Kedy Kristal, 'Competitive tendering', in *WESNET National Conference Proceedings, Women and Children Escaping Violence—Strategies into the Millennium*, WESNET, 1997, pp. 48–50.

43 *WPDO, Annual Report, 1997–1998*, p. 1.

44 Glenda Blake, interviewed by Suellen Murray, 29 July 1998.

45 Maureen Hatton, interviewed by Suellen Murray, 20 June 2000 (further comments attributed to Hatton are from this source).

46 ibid.

47 Robert J. Donovan, Donna Paterson & Mark Francas, 'Targeting male perpetrators of intimate partner violence: Western Australia's "Freedom from Fear" Campaign', *Social Marketing Quarterly*, vol. 5, no. 3, 1999, p. 127.

48 ibid.

49 ibid.

50 Leonie Gibbons, DVPU, correspondence, 1 March 2002.

51 Lesley Laing, 'Progress, trends and challenges in Australian responses to domestic violence', *Issues Paper 1*, Sydney, Australian Domestic and Family Violence Clearinghouse, 2000, p. 10. See also PADV, *MetaEvaluation*, Bulletin no. 3, February 2000, for a review of Australian programs; Leonie Gibbons, DVPU, correspondence, 3 September 2001.

52 Hatton interview.

53 See Jan Breckenridge, 'Subjugation and silences: The role of the professions in silencing victims of sexual and domestic violence', in Breckenridge & Laing (eds), *Challenging Silence*.

54 WPO, 'Women in Western Australia, Fact Sheet', 4th edn, Perth, WA Government, 1999.

55 Donovan, Paterson & Francas, 'Targeting male perpetrators', p. 136.

56 DVPU, WPDO, 'Freedom from Fear' Campaign Against Domestic Violence, *Campaign Information Sheet 1: Development of the Campaign Advertising Strategy*, Perth, WA Government, 1998.

57 'Funding for men's and women's counselling services', *DVPU News*, November 1999.

58 Gibbons, correspondence, 2001.

59 Peta Rasdien, 'Police aim at partner attacks', *West Australian*, 29 April 2000, p. 12.

60 See, for example, Victoria Wardlaw, 'Building Opportunities and Self-sufficiency', Report of the 1999 Western Australian Women's Fellowship, 2000, pp. 6–8; Hatton interview.

Notes to Conclusion: Doing themselves out of a job?

1 Lois Gatley, interviewed by Suellen Murray, 17, 29 February 2000.

2 Deborah Dearnley, interviewed by Suellen Murray, 15 May 1998.

3 FCS, *Annual Report 2000/2001*, Perth, WA Government, 2001, p. 42.

4 FCS, *Annual Report, 1997/98*, Perth, WA Government, 1997, p. 9.

5 Kedy Kristal, interviewed by Suellen Murray, 28 June 2000 (further comments attributed to Kristal are from this source).

6 DPMC, OSW, *A Say, a Choice, a Fair Go: The Government's National Agenda for Women*, Canberra, AGPS, 1988, p. 67.

7 WA Government, *Taking Action: Domestic Violence Programs and Policies*, Perth, WA Government, 1992, p. 3.

8 PADV, *First Report of the Taskforce, 1998–1999*, Canberra, Commonwealth of Australia, 1999, p. 1.

9 ABS, *Women's Safety Australia*, catalogue no. 4128.0, 1996, p. 50.

10 WPDO, *Building on Success: Government Two Year Plan for Women, 1999–2001*, vol. 1, Perth, WA Government, p. 3.

11 Cited in Juanita Doorey, 'Community liaison update', *GP News and Views*, June 2000, p. 19.

12 Coordinator's Report, *Nardine Wimmin's Refuge Annual Report 2000/2001*.

13 Dale Bagshaw, Donna Chung, Murray Couch, Sandra Lilburn & Ben Wadham, *Reshaping Responses to Domestic Violence: Executive Summary*, Adelaide, University of South Australia, 1999, p. 5.

14 Based on research conducted by the Commonwealth Government, 1987–88, and cited in Office of the Family, 'What Australians believe about domestic violence', *Domestic Violence Information Kit*, Perth, WA Government, 1990. See also DVCC, *Report to the Community*, Perth, WA Government, 1990, p. 18.

15 OSW, DPMC, *Community Attitudes to Violence Against Women*, Canberra, AGPS, 1995, p. 16.

16 Donovan Research Marketing and Communications, *Abuse in the Family, Baseline Survey: A Report to the Department for Community Development*, Perth, 1994, cited in Taskforce on Families in Western Australia, *WA Families, Our Future: Report of the Taskforce on Families in Western Australia*, Perth, WA Government, 1995, p. 163.

17 DVPU, *Freedom from Fear: Background Information Document*, Perth, WA Government, 1998, p. 9.

18 Anne McMurray, Irene Froyland, Duane Bell & David Curnow, 'Post-separation violence: The male perspective', *Journal of Family Studies*, vol. 6, no. 1, 2000, pp. 96–7.

19 Legal Aid Western Australia, *'I Just Want to be Left in Peace': Domestic Violence Legal Unit Inaugural Report*, Perth, Legal Aid, 1996, p. 18.

20 ibid.

21 ibid.

22 ibid., p. 19.

23 *Report of Chief Justice's Taskforce on Gender Bias*, Perth, WA Government, 1994; WPDO and Ministry of Justice, *Gender Bias Taskforce Progress Report*, Perth, WA Government, 1997.

24 OSW, DPMC, *Working Together Against Violence: The First Three Years of Partnerships Against Domestic Violence*, Canberra, Commonwealth of Australia, 2001, p. v.

25 Marilyn Palmer, 'Relationships in the healing century', *International Review of Women and Leadership*, Special Issue, 1999, pp. 78–86. See also Robyn Holder, '"Playing on the Football Field": Domestic Violence, Help-seeking and Community Development', paper to the Relationships Australia (NSW) 50th Anniversary Conference, Sydney, 1998; and Liz Kelly, 'Tensions and possibilities: Enhancing informal responses to domestic violence', in J. L. Edelson & Z. C. Eisikovits (eds), *Future Interventions with Battered Women and their Families*, Thousand Oaks, Sage, 1996, pp. 67–86, for further discussion of community development responses to domestic violence.

26 Judyth Watson, interviewed by Suellen Murray, 9 December 1999.

27 Anna Spencer (pseudonym), interviewed by Suellen Murray, 17 March 1998.

28 Maggie Lawson (pseudonym), interviewed by Suellen Murray, 3 March 1998.

# Select bibliography

**Abbreviations used in Bibliography**

| | |
|---|---|
| AGPS | Australian Government Publishing Service |
| DVPU | Domestic Violence Prevention Unit |
| NSW | New South Wales |
| UWA | University of Western Australia |
| WA | Western Australia/Western Australian |
| WESNET | Women's Emergency Services Network |
| WRG | Women's Refuge Group |

**Primary sources**
*All oral history interviews conducted by the author, and held by her, unless otherwise indicated*

Abdullah, Rahimah, 16 January 2001.

Allen, Sue, 5 June 1998.

Best, Libby, 26 January 1998.

Blake, Glenda, 29 July 1998.

Dearnley, Deborah, 15 May 1998.

Digby, Linda, 6 August 1998.

Elliott, Lyla, 2 March 2001.

Fatin, Wendy, interviewed by Sally Speed, 10 August 1982, Battye Library, OH1105.

Gatley, Lois, 17, 29 February 2000.

Giles, Pat, 6 April 2000.

—— interviewed by Sally Speed, 10 August 1982, Battye Library, OH1105.

Groves, Joan, 9 March 1998.
Hallahan, Kay, 7 December 1999.
Hartwig, Angie (WRG), 19 December 2000.
Hatton, Maureen, 20 June 2000.
Kagi, Carole (DVPU), 27 June 2000.
Kosky, Michele, 17 March 1998.
—— interviewed by Pascale Gilham, May 1997, private collection.
Kristal, Kedy, 28 June 2000.
Lawson, Maggie (pseudonym), 3 March 1998.
Munro, Cath, 6 June 1998.
Scott, Michelle, 7 December 1999.
Smith, Daphne, 26 May 1998.
Spencer, Anna (pseudonym), 17 March 1998.
Strong, Susie, 16 June 1998.
Warnock, Diana, 5 October 1999.
Watson, Judyth, 9 December 1999.

## Secondary sources

Allbrook, M., *Break the Cycle: The Extent and Effects on Young People of Witnessing Domestic Violence*, Perth, Youth Affairs Council of Western Australia, 1992.

Allen, J., 'The invention of the pathological family: A historical study of family violence in New South Wales', in C. O'Donnell & J. Craney (eds), *Family Violence in Australia*, Melbourne, Longman Cheshire, 1982.

Anderson, M., '"Helpmeet for man": Women in mid-nineteenth century Western Australia', in P. Crawford (ed.), *Exploring Women's Past*, Melbourne, Sisters Publishing, 1983.

Australian Bureau of Statistics, *Women's Safety Australia*, catalogue no. 4128.0, 1996.

Bagshaw, D. & Chung, D., *Women, Men and Domestic Violence*, University of South Australia, 2000.

Bagshaw, D., Chung, D., Couch, M., Lilburn, S. & Wadham, B., *Reshaping Responses to Domestic Violence: Executive Summary*, University of South Australia, 1999.

Billing-Smith, C., 'A woman's place', *Community Quarterly*, no. 36, 1995.

Blanchard, A., *Caring for Child Victims of Domestic Violence*, Perth, Nardina Press, 1999.

Breckenridge, J. & Laing, L. (eds), *Challenging Silence: Innovative Responses to Sexual and Domestic Violence*, Sydney, Allen & Unwin, 1999.

Chesterman, C., *Homes Away from Home: Supported Accommodation Assistance Program Review*, Canberra, AGPS, 1988.

Domestic Violence Coordinating Committee, *Report to the Community*, Perth, WA Government, 1990.

Domestic Violence Prevention Unit, *Best Practice Model for the Provision of Programs for Victims of Domestic Violence in Western Australia*, Perth, WA Government, 1999.

—— *Best Practice Model for the Provision of Programs for Perpetrators of Domestic Violence in Western Australia*, Perth, WA Government, 1999.

Domestic Violence Task Force, *Break the Silence*, Perth, WA Government, 1986.

Donovan, R. J., Paterson, D. & Francas, M., 'Targeting male perpetrators of intimate partner violence: Western Australia's "Freedom from Fear" campaign', *Social Marketing Quarterly*, vol. 5, no. 3, 1999.

Ellery, F., *Costs of Domestic Violence: New South Wales Domestic Violence Strategic Plan*, Sydney, NSW Women's Coordination Unit, 1991.

Evans, R., 'A gun in the oven: Masculinism and gendered violence', in K. Saunders & R. Evans (eds), *Gender Relations in Australia: Domination and Negotiation*, Sydney, Harcourt Brace, 1992.

Family and Domestic Violence Taskforce, *'It's Not Just a Domestic': An Action Plan on Family and Domestic Violence,* Perth, WA Government, 1995.

Family Violence Professional Education Taskforce, *Family Violence: Everybody's Business, Somebody's Life*, Sydney, Federation Press, 1994.

Ferrante, A., Morgan, F., Indermaur, D. & Harding, R., *Measuring the Extent of Domestic Violence*, Sydney, Hawkins Press, 1996.

FitzRoy, L., 'Just outcomes for women? State responses to violence against women', in L. Hancock (ed.), *Women, Public Policy and the State*, Melbourne, Macmillan, 1999.

Gatley, L., 'Women's rights are human rights—and that means in the home as well as community', in J. M. Barker (ed.), *Proceedings of the International Conference: Expanding Choices for Women—Health, Work and Human Rights*, Perth, John Curtin International Institute, 1997.

Grellier, M., 'The family: Some aspects of its demography and ideology in mid-nineteenth century Western Australia', in T. Stannage (ed.), *A New History of Western Australia*, Perth, UWA Press, 1981.

Hatty, S. E. (ed.), *National Conference on Domestic Violence*, Canberra, Australian Institute of Criminology, 1985.

Healy, J., 'Averting the public gaze: Social work's response to battered wives', *Australian Social Work*, vol. 37, no. 2, 1984.

Henderson, M., *Impacts and Costs of Domestic Violence on the Australian Business/Corporate Sector*, Brisbane, Lord Mayor's Women's Advisory Committee, 2000.

Holder, R., 'Domestic and family violence: Criminal justice interventions', *Issues Paper 3*, Sydney, Australian Domestic and Family Violence Clearinghouse, 2001.

Johnson, V., *The Last Resort: A Women's Refuge*, Melbourne, Penguin, 1981.

Kelly, L., 'Tensions and possibilities: Enhancing informal responses to domestic violence', in J. L. Edelson & Z. C. Eisikovits (eds), *Future Interventions with Battered Women and their Families*, Thousand Oaks, Sage, 1996.

Kristal, K., 'Competitive tendering', in *WESNET National Conference Proceedings, Women and Children Escaping Violence—Strategies into the Millennium*, Canberra, WESNET, 1997.

Laing, L., 'Progress, trends and challenges in Australian responses to domestic violence', *Issues Paper 1*, Sydney, Australian Domestic and Family Violence Clearinghouse, 2000.

—— 'Children, young people and domestic violence', *Issues Paper 2*, Sydney, Australian Domestic and Family Violence Clearinghouse, 2000.

Lake, M., *Getting Equal: The History of Australian Feminism*, Sydney, Allen & Unwin, 1999.

Legal Aid, Western Australia, *'I Just Want to be Left in Peace': Domestic Violence Legal Unit Inaugural Report*, Perth, Legal Aid, 1996.

Lyons, M., Nyland, J. & Saunders, S., 'Moving in from the fringe', in F. D. Perlmutter (ed.), *Women and Social Change: Nonprofit and Social Policy*, Washington, NASW Press, 1994.

McFerran, L., *Beyond the Image: Women's Emergency Services Programme Evaluation*, Perth, WA Government, 1987.

McFerren, L., 'Interpretation of a frontline state: Australian women's refuges and the state', in S. Watson (ed.), *Playing the State: Australian Feminist Interventions*, Sydney, Allen & Unwin, 1990.

McFerrin, L., 'Domestic violence—stories, scandals and serious analysis', *Refracting Voices: Refractory Girl*, 44/45, 1993.

McGregor, H. & Hopkins, A., *Working for Change: The Movement against Domestic Violence*, Sydney, Allen & Unwin, 1991.

National Committee on Violence Against Women, *National Strategy on Violence Against Women*, Canberra, Commonwealth of Australia, 1992.

Noesjirwan, J., 'Ten years on: A review of women's refuges in New South Wales', in S. E. Hatty (ed.), *National Conference on Domestic Violence*, Canberra, Australian Institute of Criminology, 1985.

Office of the Status of Women, Department of Prime Minister and Cabinet, *Working Together Against Violence: The First Three Years of Partnerships Against Domestic Violence*, Canberra, Commonwealth of Australia, 2001.

—— *Community Attitudes to Violence against Women*, Canberra, AGPS, 1995.

Orr, L., 'The women's refuge movement in Victoria', in W. Weeks (ed.), *Women Working Together: Lessons from Feminist Women's Services*, Melbourne, Longman Cheshire, 1994.

Otto, D. & Haley, E., 'Helter shelter: A history of the Adelaide women's shelter', *Refractory Girl*, Winter, 1975.

Palmer, M., 'Relationships in the healing century', *International Review of Women and Leadership*, Special Issue, 1999.

Partnerships Against Domestic Violence, *First Report of the Taskforce, 1998–1999*, Canberra, Commonwealth of Australia, 1999.

Pizzey, E., *Scream Quietly or the Neighbours Will Hear*, Melbourne, Penguin, 1974.

Rooney, K., 'Dealing with domestic violence in WA', *Legal Service Bulletin*, vol. 8, no. 5, 1983.

Saunders, K., 'The study of domestic violence in colonial Queensland: Sources and problems', *Historical Studies*, vol. 21, 1984.

Saville, H., 'Refuges: A new beginning to the struggle', in C. O'Donnell & J. Craney (eds), *Family Violence in Australia*, Melbourne, Longman Cheshire, 1982.

Scutt, J., *Even in the Best of Homes: Violence in the Family*, Melbourne, Penguin, 1983.

Weeks, W., 'Towards the prevention of violence and the creation of safe and supportive gender relations', in W. Weeks & M. Quinn (eds), *Issues Facing Australian Families: Human Services Respond*, 3rd edn, Sydney, Longman, 2000.

—— *Women Working Together: Lessons from Feminist Women's Services*, Melbourne, Longman Cheshire, 1994.

Weeks, W. & Gilmore, K., 'How violence against women became an issue on the national policy agenda', in T. Dalton, M. Draper, W. Weeks & J. Wiseman (eds), *Making Social Policy in Australia: An Introduction*, Sydney, Allen & Unwin, 1996.

Western Australian Government, *Taking Action: Domestic Violence Programs and Policies*, Perth, WA Government, 1992.

# Index